Nooks Crannies and Corners

Learning Centers for Creative Classrooms

A KIDS' STUFF BOOK

by Imogene Forte and Joy Mackenzie

A
KIDS' STUFF
BOOK

Library of Congress # 77-92968
ISBN #0-913916-55-2

Revised Edition

To our husbands
Henry and Bob

Preface

NOOKS, CRANNIES AND CORNERS: Learning Centers for Creative Classrooms was written for teachers, administrators and teachers-to-be. The authors hoped that it would also assist parents and interested laymen in gaining insights into the learning center approach to classroom instruction.

It was not intended to be a scholarly or comprehensive analysis of the individualization process or a recipe for a super-teacher in the individualized classroom. It was designed to serve as a handbook written by teachers to provide other teachers with a simple, easy-to-follow outline and guide for planning and using learning centers.

It was originally developed as a result of dialogue with hundreds of teachers, students, administrators and parents who felt the need to move toward a "personalization" of the learning experience. The need for practical patterns and guidelines to follow while moving from conventional teaching techniques to those that would more closely provide for the uniqueness in individual pupils' abilities and learning behaviors was expressed over and over again.

Now, five years later, after a careful review of the literature and interviews with teachers, parents and students from coast to coast, we find that the excitement generated by the learning center approach is still very much with us. Creative and resourceful teachers in all types of classrooms are utilizing learning centers in all shapes, sizes, styles and varying levels of sophistication. While it is still difficult to arrive at one fixed definition of exactly what constitutes a learning center, there is a consensus that learning centers have indeed made a significant contribution to humanistic education.

The content of NOOKS, CRANNIES AND CORNERS has been carefully reviewed, revised and significantly expanded to bring the ideas, suggestions and work sheets up to date, and to make them practical for teachers who need help in launching, carrying on or expanding a learning center approach to classroom instruction.

Again, it is to those teachers who are willing to be honest, who share a sense of wonder and curiosity about the world and who find delight in helping children learn—to those who believe in themselves, in the intrinsic value and unique worth of a single human being—to those who love living and learning, that this book is offered with renewed excitement and enthusiasm.

Imogene Forte
Joy MacKenzie

Nashville, Tennessee
1978

CONTENTS

Individualize—
That's Some Order!

Individualize—That's Some Order!

"Meeting individual needs" has become a well-known cliché in the present day educators' vocabularly, but it is seldom a comfortable one. The idea of meeting the learners' needs on a one-to-one basis is compelling, if not a mandatory educational assumption, but there looms overhead that inevitable ominous cloud of doubt that in practical reality we can exercise that which we so firmly believe.

The task of personalizing instruction assumes a whole new dimension as soon as it moves from the college textbook to the live classroom. There the spectrum of needs and abilities to be dealt with is as wide as the number of children; and the dilemma is magnified by the real limitations of time, space, staff, resources and energy.

The "process" of individualization appears, at the least, a formidable, if not portentous undertaking. And it can become less threatening only if we stop referring to it as *something to be done to* students and begin regarding it as *a way of thinking* about learning and learners. Truly, it demands of us the best that we are and have to offer in terms of knowledge of content and method, organization, instructional strategies, and understanding of the nature and behavior of learners and the learning process.

But more significant is the intimate, personal de-

3

mand it places upon us as human beings. For with the commitment to "individualize" we have designed to grant to the learner the *right* to individuality. We have released him from the shackles he sustained as a mere receiver of information and performer of assigned tasks. Suddenly, we have accorded to him the freedom to initiate, to respond, to choose, to create, to direct, and along with those lofty concessions, the right to ask unsettling questions, to come up with disturbing answers, to doubt the worth of cherished practices, to consider "unthinkable alternatives."

The suggestion is that our dilemma is not one of capability so much as one of willingness—not so much a question of commitment to an ideal as it is a matter of gathering courage to deal with the exceptional, the inventive, the unpredictable.

We are menaced by the fear of creating a monster— or perhaps that is only the rationalization behind which we hide our insecurities about ourselves. When we begin to think of the learner as a single, unique human being, apart from comparable denomination or classification, we begin to see his learning problems in a different light. No longer can we excuse failure as "immaturity" or "inability" on the learner's part. Rather we must accept it as an immaturity in the development of the teaching skills and abilities which would allow us to find a way to free him from his learning problems.

Individualize—that's some order! Give a teacher 36 students in a 20′x30′ classroom, the same old furniture, the same old books, few old and no new materials and tell him to get the job done. . . .

While you're giving orders, don't forget to mention that he needs to take personal inventory of his very being and become the kind of person who can relate to and live with the individualization process. Be sure that he is familiar with and able to employ consistent diagnostic procedures designed to isolate and clarify differences in students' abilities and readiness stages. Don't neglect to point out that he must be ready to plan and coordinate a multi-phasic program of tasks, experiences and opportunities related to specific, realistic curriculum goals, and have at his disposal multiple choices for methods, procedures and strategies for presenting those skills and concepts his pupils need and are ready to gain. . . . AND provide at the same time a horizontal flexibility that promotes independence in decision-making and self-direction and allows for unlimited alternatives and personal choices by his pupils. You might also check his prowess as a gymnast in the arrangement of time and space and caution him that he will be expected to provide both immediate and long-term evaluative criteria and keep records strong enough for court evidence to parents, unbelieving colleagues and administrators that his pupils are making as good or better progress than they might be making in a traditional classroom.

If by this time he is still interested in individualizing instruction for his students, suggest that he consider the learning center approach as a means to this end.

So Exactly What Is
A Learning Center?

So exactly what is a learning center?

Any place on earth (or elsewhere) where learning can abound! In terms of the school classroom, a learning center is merely a physical area where children engage in a variety of learning activities and experiences.

The character and design of learning centers may vary greatly in order to provide the kinds of space, materials, and method of content-presentation needed to accommodate the experiences or tasks peculiar to the content of each center.

Are there any characteristics common to all learning centers?

Very few—but very important ones!

1. A learning center must include multi-level activities or experiences to meet the instructional needs of every child who will visit the center.

2. A learning center must offer choices and alternatives in the tasks it requires, giving every student a part in planning and executing his own learning; thus his *personal* interests and needs become a part of the curriculum rather than a predetermined curriculum becoming an enforced part of him.

3. Factors which greatly and directly influence the success of a center are:

   • Its neatness and attractiveness.

—Is it a pleasant, comfortable place to work?

—Is it beckoning—from across the room?

- Its immediate motivational qualities.

—Does it arouse curiosity, perhaps offer a hint of intrigue?

—Does it capitalize on personal and group interests?

—Is there any good reason a student should be anxious to work there?

- The clarity and simplicity with which procedures are outlined or directions are given.

—Can directions be easily read and understood without difficulty, allowing tasks to be easily effected without additional help from the teacher?

- The quality and apparent value to the student of its evaluative devices.

—Are the provisions for self-evaluation precise and purposeful enough to provide meaningful information to both student and teacher?

Are there any other "rules-of-thumb" for developing successful centers?

Here are some that many teachers have found helpful:

1. Center activities may or may not be ordered for sequential development.

2. Experiences may be designed to be enjoyed by individual students or by two or three—or perhaps as many as six students working together.

3. Effective use of a center is more often than not facilitated by an initial presentation or explanation of the new center's intended purpose and operational procedures. This introduction may be made by the teacher or by pupils.

4. Time limitations may be imposed for the use of each center, but these must remain flexible enough to make allowances for the pupils who will need more time, and yet encourage efficient performance in all pupils.

5. The number of pupils who may visit a given center at one time may be an appropriate decision for students to make as a network of "ground rules" for efficient use of centers.

   NOTE: Permanent ground rules may govern the use of some centers. On the other hand, any new center may require new decisions related to its use.

6. Movement to and from or between centers must be well-coordinated with other activities in the instructional program.

   (In areas of limited space, a definite traffic pattern or right-of-way system may have to be specified.)

7. Execution of center activities is not necessarily limited to the physical area designated as the learning center. In many instances, students may be directed to other areas in or outside of the classroom for completion of activities.

8. Life, vitality and enthusiasm for a given center are engendered by *change*. Some centers will change every day, others once a week. Still others may remain constant for a longer period. It is expedient, however, to keep in mind that in a learning center society, neither tradition nor "old age" is cherished or revered.

9. Variety is the spice of life—an old adage, but a wise one. When several centers are in use in one classroom, careful attention must be given to the balance of design in centers.

   - Some provide for *active* involvement, others for more *quiet* activity.

   - Some require only short attention, others demand time for long-term development.

   - Some offer experiences in reading and writing; others will be non-verbal in their design.

   - Some are designed for individual work, others for the cooperative efforts of pairs or small groups.

   - Some will be open-ended and experimental in nature; others will be more structured in presentation of content.

- Some may be completely pupil-structured (yes, even unedited by the teacher!) and others totally prepared by the teacher.

10. At each center which does not, by nature, provide for individual ability level and freedom of choice, a system will need to be developed for indicating what activities and alternatives are reserved to which students.

How does one develop a "system" for assignment of center activities?

One of two ways: follow a tried and true system already classroom tested, (a few are suggested in the appendix—"Signs, Symbols, and Secret Codes") OR devise your own!

Any plan that a teacher and his students can devise and implement to their satisfaction and facility is the best one for them.

There is no very effective way for a textbook to write prescriptions for individual classrooms. Unfortunately, the best *it* can do is *suggest* or offer alternatives.

Classroom experience has taught the authors that the most valuable resource for finding solutions to these kinds of problems—and perhaps most problems encountered in teaching—is the student. That reservoir is seldom disappointing in its yield!

How is a learning center born?

As its parallels in life, a learning center may be conceived with ease and enthusiasm, but it is seldom born without labor and concern.

Ah—that brings it down to basic terms! Let's state the actual task in four direct questions:

1. *What* do I want the child to be able to *do* in order to show that he *understands the idea or concept* taught?

   ### OR

   What task do I want him to be able to perform in order to show that he has *mastered the skill* presented?

2. What *tools and materials* will I need to provide in order for him to do this?

3. What *directions, guidelines* and *explanations* are necessary for him to be able to accomplish this task?

   (How can I most simply and efficiently help him go about it?)

4. How will I know *if* and *how well* he has accomplished the task?

   (How will *he* know when he has been successful?)

If you just said to yourself, "Ha. What's 'learning center' about that? That's just like a plain old traditional lesson plan!" You're exactly right! Of course!

Learning centers are not new ways of teaching. They just represent one good method of organizing content and materials to make learning easier and more enjoyable for some children!

 NOTE: See appendix, Part I: A PLAN FOR DEVELOPING A LEARNING CENTER; also, **Model Outline of a Learning Center**

    a. pre-school level

    b. primary level

    c. intermediate level
       at the end of this chapter.

Is there more than one kind of learning center?

As many kinds as there are kids . . . and teachers.

Centers are rather like people. They have personalities, if you please. Each takes on the character of its progenitors and is influenced by its environment.

But looking at the question from a broad, organizational point of view, most learning centers will fall into one of two categories: *uni-disciplinary centers* or *multi-disciplinary centers*. Let's define those terribly traumatizing terms briefly and simply:

- A *uni-disciplinary center* is a center in which experiences and activities are confined to the teaching of one or more specific concepts related to *one content area.*

- *A multi-disciplinary center* is a center in which the experiences and activities are all related to *one topic* (i.e. birds, Texas, fractions, rhyming words, the short story, mining, composing, the human body, etc.) but provides for the integration of several or all content areas.

An outline example of each follows.

A Uni-disciplinary Center:

Content Area: Language Arts

Skill-Subject: Word Sensitivity

Sample Activities:

I. Word Box, recorded direction—"Write one descriptive word for each object in the box."

II. Ditto sheet of sentences using the verb TO SAY—Ask children to substitute a more precise word for SAY in each sentence. They choose their three *best* contributions and drop in locked box to be shared with class later.

III. Story segment illustrating the manipulation of word meaning to fit personal taste—recorded. Discussion in groups of 3-4. Make up their own sets of words.

A Multi-disciplinary Center:

Content Areas: All

Topic: "The American Revolution"

Sample Activities:

Language Arts—Letter writing to relatives still on European continent.

Math—Exercise in making estimates in relation to provisions (i.e. food, supplies, etc.)

Science—Experiment with rocks and soil—growing climate.

Social Studies—(partners or pairs) Develop debate related to a controversial issue in American thought at the time

OR

Compare American thought (political) in those times with current times. . . .

Art—(group activity) Creating junk sculpture that represents an emotion, feeling, or abstract idea common to people at the time of the revolution. . . .

Music—Individual listening activity—finding commonalities in folksongs and ballads growing out of this period of history.

Note:
A classroom may have many *uni-disciplinary centers* (perhaps one or more for each content area) which are constantly changing.
Multi-disciplinary centers change as units of study change OR may be used as in the uni-disciplinary pattern to integrate all content areas with every concept taught.

All activities in all centers would presumably have *multi-level* and *choice* alternatives.

How can I be sure to "get the curriculum covered" in a learning center setting?

Don't let it cover you! And if you teach in a school which demands a daily menu in keeping with a pre-determined diet, and you're *worried* about it, you may have a problem.

The suggestion is not to ignore the diet. Diets are developed for good reasons; they become distasteful only when they bring frustration and misery to our daily living. If we allow enthusiasm and flexibility to be overshadowed by what we see as unreasonable restraints, then perhaps our regimentation is self-imposed, and we have misinterpreted the intent of a prescribed curriculum.

It must be kept in mind that any curriculum guide or outline has been developed for the ideal or hoped-for teaching situation. It is a goal proposal for the minimum to maximum content material that may be covered in a given school year.

If this sort of outline is an expected part of your long-range planning, welcome it as a guide—and only a guide—in your design to meet the individual needs in your classroom.

• Plan centers to include the designated units of

study that promise to hold the most meaning and value for your students.

- Prepare a calendar on which you can set up an estimated time plan for introducing these centers.

- Scan proposed texts and materials carefully and decide in what capacity each can be used most worthily.

- Make initial decisions about the methods and strategies that will best facilitate the presentation of each block of content.

- Determine how students may participate in the preparations for each new endeavor AND how they might be involved in the total implementation of curriculum goals.

Is the learning center design the only way to individualize instruction?

It's the one NOOKS, CRANNIES and CORNERS is pushing, but there are others!

When we refer to individualized instruction, we are implying a move from teacher-directed, group-oriented instructional strategies. The move is directed toward providing for differences in pupils through a range of alternative learning opportunities from which prescriptive activities can be selected.

Many teachers lull themselves into a false sense of security by initiating a pseudo-individualized program.

Some of the "free" reading programs which allow students to select their own library books fall into this category. While these programs do allow for freedom of choice, they do not afford sequential growth in skill usage, nor do they necessarily foster valid appreciative development.

Some of the programmed instructional aids utilizing sophisticated hardware and supporting materials, and bandying the term "individualized instruction" also fall into this category. Differentiated staffing, open spaces or a permissive classroom atmosphere do not necessarily denote individualized instruction either.

Tutorial arrangements such as the "each-one-teach-one" method, independent study projects, and some types of commercial programs are, however, examples of approaches to individualized instruction that may well be very effective.

MODEL OUTLINE OF A LEARNING CENTER —PRESCHOOL LEVEL

CONTENT AREA: Science

TOPIC: Sound

I. Objectives

A. Central Purpose: Children should be able to demonstrate their understanding of sound as a natural phenomenon of their environment, and be able to interpret, recognize and classify sounds.

B. Specific Purposes:

Level I: Child can demonstrate his understanding of sound and his ability to "listen" to specific sounds through rhythmic movement.

Level II: Child can, with facility and accuracy, demonstrate his understanding of low, high, loud or soft sounds.

Level III: Child can recognize, identify and classify sounds of the environment.

II. Tools and Materials

Instruments that make sounds such as a bell, triangle, whistle, harmonica, spoon, squeaking toy animal, stick, tambourine, paper, crayons, cassette player and tapes, straight pins, sound boxes prepared according to directions under *Level II;* flannel board and felt-backed pictures of pictorial symbols for: bell, clock, birds, cars, feet, rain, playing, fire engine, laughing, baby crying, cooking, pencil sharpener, typewriter, airplane, dog, classroom, school, office, campus and cafeteria.

III. Operational Procedure

   A. Introduction of Center and Directions for Use:

      1. Prepare the flannel board and felt-backed pictures to be easily accessible to children.

      2. Place the pictorial symbols across the top of the board as illustrated.

      3. Explain and demonstrate use of the flannel board.

      4. Prepare instrument table and sound boxes. (Follow instructions given in operational procedure).

      5. Explain and demonstrate use of instrument table.

   B. Procedures:

   Level I:

      1. Let children go to the instrument table and experiment with instruments to discover for themselves what kind of sound each one makes. Let the "leader" of the group select one picture and ask for vounteers to demonstrate the sound that the object in the picture might make by using one or more of the instruments.

      2. Ask the children to move in the way they think the object making that particular sound might move.

Alternative: They may listen to taped sounds and interpret with bodily movement or dance the sound they hear.

Evaluation: Divide the children into groups, giving each group several pictures and instruments in accordance with which they will make their own sounds and movements. Let the other children guess the sound being demonstrated.

Level II:

1. Use taped music, with the volume of the cassette player adjusted to provide loud and then soft sounds. Have children identify loud sounds by raising both hands above their heads, and soft sounds by lowering both hands to the floor.

2. To demonstrate that sound can be high or low, make recordings using a xylophone and flute, or any two instruments of like timbre. Follow the same procedure as outlined in step one.

Alternatives: Play a game using the felt-backed pictures. Classify them by arranging them in four stacks identified as *soft, loud, high* or *low.*

OR

Play a game using instruments from the instrument table. Let one child be the "sounder" and other children put heads down and close eyes. The "sounder" moves to one part of the room, and with an instrument selected from the table, makes a sound. Blindfolded children point to where the sound is coming from. The "sounder" then says "Is it loud?" "Is it soft?" Is it high?" "Is it low?"—(Teacher may need to give help to both "sounder" and listeners the first few times this game is played.)

Evaluation: Make four "sound boxes" by covering two boxes with blue paper and two with red paper. Place on each box a symbol to indicate soft sound, loud sound, high sound and low sound. Allow children to work individually or in small groups to properly classify the instruments on the table by putting them in the correct boxes.

Level III:

1. Discuss sounds around us. (This could be taped for use with a cassette player in the center.)

2. Take a walk around the classroom, around the building and outside. Come back to the classroom and discuss what was heard.

3. Have children match pictures on the flannel board with the proper symbol to show in which part of the environment they can be found. (Help children note that some sounds can be classified under more than one category.)

Alternatives: Children may play a game by pinning a picture of a sound heard on the back of one child who does not know what the picture is. Other children give "sound" clues until he guesses what it is (or gives up). This game may continue until all children who wish a turn have been "it" or until the interest span of the group is exhausted.

OR

The group leader may hold up pictures and ask other children to supply "sound" words that are associated with the object (i.e., typewriter: snapping, clattering, banging, zinging, pecking, pinging, popping, chattering, humming).

OR

They may draw a picture including two or more things they "heard" on their walk.

Evaluation: Groups may "share" their experience with other members of the large group and check the accuracy of their perceptions through verbal feedback.

MODEL OUTLINE OF A LEARNING CENTER –PRIMARY LEVEL

CONTENT AREA: Social Studies

TOPIC: Maps

I. Objectives

   A. Central Purpose: Children should be able to demonstrate their understanding of a map as symbolic of a real place and be ble to interpret map symbols to gain information.

   B. Specific Purposes:

   Level I: Child can orient himself as to location in relation to things in his immediate environment.

   Level II: Child can demonstrate his understanding of the relativity in location of objects in the environment by making a map of a real place.

   Level III: Child can, with facility and accuracy, locate objects in terms of distance, direction, and relative location by translating given information into map form.

II. Tools and Materials

   Pencils, paper, furnished doll house, box and

model furniture, tape recorder and tape, answer boxes and maps, table, 3-4 chairs, bulletin board with symbols and pictures.

III. Operational Procedure

    A. Introduction of Center:

        1. Discuss purpose and use of maps, using map of school or classroom as an example.

        2. Explain and demonstrate use of manipulative bulletin board at center.

    B. Directions for Use:

        1. Color code

        2. Use and care of materials and equipment

        3. Appoint monitors

    C. Procedures:

        Level I: Provide low-sided box the same shape as classroom and models which represent major pieces of furniture in the real room. Ask children to arrange furniture in the model box classroom to match its placement in the real classroom.

        Alternative: He may draw a map of the room.

Evaluation: Provide an "answer box" in which identical pieces are glued for comparison.

Level II: Provide furnished doll house. Ask children to observe a room in which furniture has been previously secured. Ask them to compare room with the "map" of that room which is secured to table or roof of doll house to see similarity. Ask child to choose a second room in the house and *draw* a map which shows the location of items in that room.

Alternatives: He may make a model of the room.

OR

He may draw a map of the entire house or any other part or parts he chooses.

OR

He may draw a map of his own house or room.

Evaluation: He may check his map with an "answer map" which has been provided.

Level III: Child listens to recorded travel

story, traces movement in story on a partial map provided.

Alternatives: He may listen to second story on tape and draw his own map.

OR

He may make up travel story and add to tape.

OR

He may make a map of a trip he has taken.

Evaluation: Child checks his map with "answer map."

MODEL OUTLINE OF A LEARNING CENTER —INTERMEDIATE/JR. HIGH/ HIGH SCHOOL LEVELS

CONTENT AREA: Language Arts

SKILLS: Critical Reading
Vocabulary Enrichment
Word Usage
Creative Writing

NOTE: This would be a large center with a distinct area for each skill part. Sitting/ writing space would need to be provided for at least 8-10 students.

CRITICAL READING

I. Objectives

A. Central Purpose: Students should be able to recognize and interpret hidden "intent" or "inference" in written communication.

B. Specific Purposes:

Level I: Students can recognize and isolate words intended to create emotional appeal.

Level II: Students can associate recognized intentions and inferences with the human needs and emotions to which they appeal and are able to create like appeals through written communication.

Level III: Students are able to make personal judgments about the worth and morality of attempt to deceive through the medium of public advertising.

II. Tools and Materials

Four or five large, attractive magazine ads, mounted and displayed on a bulletin board or protected in acetate sheets and placed in a box or envelope; paper, pencils, scissors, paste, plain and colored construction paper; large, empty board space where students can display original ads.

III. Operational Procedure

A. Introduction of Center Area and Directions for Use:

1. Discuss general purpose and use of advertising; go over all instructions.

2. Point out art supplies and empty board space for original displays.

3. Ask students to make suggestions about how original ads may be used for evaluative purposes. Schedule a future time to make final decision related to this.

B. Procedures:

Level I: Ask student to choose *words* from the ads that make the reader want to "buy" and list them on paper.

OR

He may write a sentence about each ad, telling how it makes him *feel*.

Optional: He may design his own ad for an imaginary product, place it on the board and see how many "buyers" he can attract.

Evaluation: Written work; optional work, group decision.

Level II: Ask student to read ads and make a list of the human emotions or needs to which they appeal.

OR

He may make up three ads of his own which use the same psychology or emotional appeal as three of the displayed ads.

Optional: Same as *Level I*

Evaluation: Written work; optional work, group decision.

Level III: Ask student to read ads and write a sentence explaining real *intent* of each ad.

AND/OR

Take a position: "With which of the following statements do you agree? Write a paragraph to explain your choice."

1. Advertisers should be required by law to be totally honest; they should not be permitted to use subtle deceit to sell products to the general public.

2. America is a "free-press" society. Advertisers ought to be allowed to print anything they wish; if the public is deceived, it is its own fault for not buying cautiously.

Optional: Same as *Level I.*

Evaluation: Written work; optional, group decision.

VOCABULARY ENRICHMENT

I. Objectives

A. Central Purpose: Students should be able to use descriptive words with increasing sensitivity and preciseness.

B. Specific Purposes:

Levels I and II: Students can demonstrate sensitivity and preciseness in the use of adjectives by matching descriptive words

with the real-life situations
which they *best* describe.

Level III: Students can demonstrate
skill in making word associ-
ations and drawing infer-
ences by choosing from
many possible life-situations
the one *best* described by
each of 10 sentences.

II. Tools and Materials

Six or seven large, colorful pictures demonstrating
human emotion (numbered 1-7); bulletin board
space or substitute; pencil, paper, 3″ x 5″ cards,
tacks or tape; six or seven envelopes—one attached behind or below each picture;

Level I: 10-12 word cards bearing adjectives
which can be associated with chosen
pictures—i.e., *angry, sad, embarrassed, disgusted, overjoyed, anxious, im-
patient, excited,* etc.

Level II: 10-12 word cards—same as *Level I*
with more difficult words (i.e., *furious,
harassed, exuberant, amorous, ex-
hilarated, implacable, arrogant,* etc.)

Level III: 10-15 cards bearing sentences which
describe, by inference, the emotions
displayed by the pictures. (i.e., *"Se-
rious consequences follow infraction of*

rules." "*Feelings are not often camou-*
flaged by facial expression." "*Inge-*
nious minds excel in clever design."
etc.)

III. Operational Procedure

    A. Introduction of Center Area and Directions
       for Use:

       1. Locate all materials and demonstrate use
          of word and sentence cards.

       2. Give directions for adding cards to en-
          velopes.

       3. Ask students to think, as they work at the
          center, about ways in which the envelopes
          of collected word cards might be used
          to evaluate skills in preciseness of word
          choice and in word sensitivity. Set a future
          time for making suggestions.

    B. Procedures:

      Level I: Ask child to match each *Level I*
                 word card with the mounted pic-
                 ture it *best* describes and explain
                 his choices to a friend.

                         OR

                 He may number the pictures on
                 paper and list the words he
                 matched with each picture; discuss
                 choices with friend or teacher.

Required: He must, on a 3″x 5″ card, write an additional word of his own for each picture and insert it in the envelope below each corresponding picture.

Level II: Same as *Level I,* substituting *Level II* word cards.

Level III: Same as *Level I* and *II,* substituting *Level III* sentence cards.

Evaluation—All Levels: Group decision

WORD USAGE

I. Objectives

  A. General Objective: Students should be able to recognize and classify words according to their uses in the context of a sentence.

  B. Specific Objectives:

    Level I: Students can recognize and use verbs and adjectives in context.

    Levels II and III: Students can recognize and classify nouns, verbs, adjectives and adverbs according to their uses in context.

II. Tools and Materials

  Level I: Duplicated sheets of a list of 10 simple nouns.

Levels II and III: Duplicated sheets bearing the following paragraph:

Horskly, the minkled gooks kittled. The murks skorked the grunches and rittled the morks. The runches gloored skatily, and the grimped gottles griffled. The mak mootled mortily.

All: pencils, crayons, paper.

III. Operational Procedure

    A. Introduction of Center Area and Directions for Use:

        1. Define *noun, verb, adjective, adverb* and discuss examples of each with group.

        2. Identify materials and read all directions; answer any questions.

    B. Procedures:

      Level I: Ask student to locate the duplicated list of 10 nouns. *Before* each noun, he is to write a *descriptive* word that makes sense. *After* each noun, he is to add an *action* word that makes sense. Then he should read each phrase to himself.

OR

He may write 3 original sentences, each containing a noun, verb, and adjective. He may classify the words by *circling* all verbs and *underlining* all adjectives.

Evaluation: Written work—number of words
used or classified properly.

Level II: Ask student to obtain duplicated
nonsense story. He must classify all
nouns, verbs, adjectives, and ad-
verbs by using a color code of his
own. (Remind him to add a color
key, so that his classification may
be understood.)

OR

He may write five original sentences, using *real* words, and classify all four kinds of words by list-
ing them under the headings:
NOUN — VERB—ADJECTIVE
—ADVERB at the bottom of his
paper.

Evaluation: Written work—number of words
properly classified.

Level III: Same as *Level II*

OR

Student may compose original story
of *nonsense* words and classify
nouns, verbs, adjectives and ad-
verbs by any method he chooses to
devise.

Evaluation: Written work—number of words
properly classified.

CREATIVE WRITING

I. Objectives

    A. General Objective: Student will be able to demonstrate skills in association, transference and writing style by translating, either from reading or memory, a fable or folktale into a present-day journalistic-style news or feature story.

II. Tools and Materials

An abbreviated form of the story "Rip Van Winkle" and a model report of that story as it might appear in the news or feature section of a local newspaper if "Rip" had been discovered just this week. Duplicated copies of a similar folktale, paper, pencil; duplicating masters—optional.

III. Operational Procedure

    A. Introduction of Center and Directions for Use:

        1. Identify materials, review directions.

        2. Discuss "journalistic" style—as compared with ordinary prose. Mention the key words *Who—What—When—Where* and

added *items of human and public interest* (and *opinion*, in feature stories).

3. Discuss how the *optional* activity might be best accomplished. Set a time for those who choose that activity to make final decisions.

B. Procedures:

All Levels: Ask student to read abbreviated story of "Rip Van Winkle" and its corresponding model of a modern-day news or feature story.

Ask him then to read a second similar story, chosen by the teacher and write a corresponding modern-day news or feature account of the story in journalistic style.

OR

He may do the same assignment using a folktale of his own choosing.

Optional: Any student may submit his story for publication in a local class newspaper. The process of collecting, preparing and duplicating the paper will be determined by a committee of those electing to participate.

You've got to be joking! What teacher in this world has time to develop learning centers which are so complex and complicated?

Well, it's like painting a picture with oil paints or making a great omelet—you have to learn by the rules so that you can depart to do your own thing in a truly creative sense.

You probably will neither want or need to make such detailed plans or elaborate center activity programming as we have presented in the model outlines. The same amount of time and effort you devote to unit teaching and/or day-to-day lesson plans should suffice for learning center teaching. The important thing to remember is that the keys to success are careful organization of materials and instructions, realistic expectations and provisions for student options.

In addition to the carefully planned learning center, are there other kinds of centers that can be used to individualize instruction?

You should be awarded the "Teacher of the Day" prize for asking that question.

The effectiveness of planned instructional learning centers is enhanced immensely when it is reinforced and extended through the use of mini-centers, skills activity centers and free-choice interest centers.

So what's a mini-center?

Thought you'd never ask!

A mini-center is a simple, concise programming of instructional materials to be used by one particular student to develop one particular skill or concept. Mini-centers need to be totally self-contained and include all the instructions, materials and tools necessary for completion of the activities. The grand feature of mini-centers is that they may be taken to the student's desk, to the playground or even home. Instructions should be simple and easily understood so that no teacher help is required. Unusual containers related to the mini-center theme add interest and provide motivation. Many mini-centers will be a viable asset to any classroom teacher attempting to individualize instruction.

NOTE: Two model mini-centers may be found on the following pages. For additional mini-center ideas—perhaps more than you ever wanted, be sure to see MINI-CENTER STUFF by Forte and Pangle. This all-inclusive book presents sixty-nine model centers, each built around a central theme and offering math, language arts and environmental activities as well as a related, "just-for-fun" project.

Make It Metric!

Purpose: Using Metric Measurements

Preparation Directions:

1. Cover a sturdy square cardboard box with white shelf paper.
2. Place the following items in the box:
    1) metric tape measure
    2) metric ruler
    3) three Celsius thermometers
    4) metric measuring cup
    5) pencil
    6) writing paper
    7) crayons
    8) newspaper
    9) keys for tasks
    10) activities (see separate activities for materials needed)
    11) metric study guide
3. Print these directions on an index card and tape to the side of the box.
    "Follow the directions and complete the tasks. Evaluate completed activities with the teacher."

Activities:

1. Print metric terms on one piece of poster board. Punch a hole beside each metric term. Attach yarn to each hole. Print metric abbreviations on another piece of poster board. Punch a hole beside each metric abbreviation.

Print the following directions on the back of the piece of poster board on which the metric terms are printed.

"Attach the yarn from the metric term to the metric abbreviation. Use the key to check the answers."

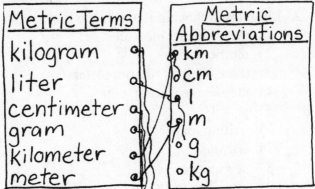

2. Print the following directions on an index card and place in the metric measuring cup.

"A metric cup holds 250 milliliters. Take the cup to a sink to measure water and complete the task."

    _____ cups = 1 liter
    _____ cups = 2 liters
    _____ cups = ½ liter
    _____ cups = ¼ liter
    _____ cups = ¾ liter

3. Cut out items from a grocery store advertisement in the newspaper. Paste the pictures on small pieces of tagboard. Place the pictures in an envelope. Paste three envelopes on a piece

of posterboard and label the envelopes: "grams," "kilograms" and "liters." Print the following instructions on the back of the piece of posterboard.

"Look at the pictures. Place each picture in the envelope that tells how the item would be weighed metrically."

Examples: meat — kilograms
candy — grams
milk — liters

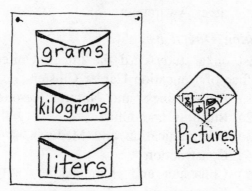

4. Cut out a shape from posterboard to resemble a thermometer. Print the following directions on the thermometer.

"Place one Celsius thermometer in the warmest spot in the classroom. Place one Celsius thermometer outside. Place one Celsius thermometer in a cup of cold water. Leave each thermometer fifteen minutes and then record the temperatures on each thermometer."

JUST FOR FUN:
Design a metric pantry. Label the items on the shelves and estimate the metric measurements for each item.
. . . and don't forget to:
Autograph the "Make It Metric" box. Record the date you completed the mini-center, and draw an object that can be measured metrically.

Career Concerns

Purpose: Career Awareness

Preparation Directions:

1. List on a study card the fifteen United States Office of Education Career Clusters:
    1) Agri-Business and Natural Resources
    2) Business and Office
    3) Communication and Media
    4) Construction
    5) Consumer and Homemaking
    6) Environment
    7) Fine Arts and Humanities
    8) Health Services
    9) Hospitality, Recreation and Leisure
    10) Manufacturing
    11) Marine Science
    12) Marketing and Distribution
    13) Personal Services
    14) Public Service
    15) Transportation

2. Make work sheets for each of the following activities.

3. Number the work sheets and place them in a manila folder labeled "Career Concerns."

4. Place the folder, the study card, a pencil, writing paper, a dictionary and a newspaper in a brief case. Make a "Career Concerns" sign for the outside of the brief case.

Activities:

1. Select the career cluster that interests you most and make a list of jobs within that cluster. List the natural talents and abilities you would need in order to pursue a career from this cluster.

2. Select one career from each of these fields. Write a one-paragraph report or prepare a series of labeled illustrations showing how the educational requirements and job descriptions for each have changed during the past fifty years (examples: nurse, kindergarten teacher, editor, carpenter, forest ranger).

      Medicine   Education
      Journalism   Construction
          Conservation

3. Read through the newspaper. Find a news story related to one career that is of interest to you. Give the following information in the space provided:

    Who _____

    What _____

When _____

Where _____

Now write an entirely different news story that could have happened within the same setting and related to the same person (or people) and the same career.

4. Find one "position available" ad in the Want Ad section of the newspaper for a position that is of interest to you. Write a letter giving your qualifications, stating why you want the job and asking for a personal interview. Don't forget to put your best foot forward by writing neatly, spelling correctly and using the proper form for a business letter.

5. Congratulations! You have been invited to interview for your dream job. Make a list of questions that you may be asked during the interview. Think carefully about the answers you will give. Plan the outfit you will wear for the interview and draw a picture of yourself dressed for this important occasion.

JUST FOR FUN:

Select one job you would like to have. Write a job description for the job as it is now, and one for what you think it will be when you enter the job market. List the major changes you think will take place and the new skills you will need to perform the job.

After all is said and done, educators and

parents still seem to agree that the teacher's most important job is to teach the three R's. How can I deal with the pressure to teach basic skills as opposed to personalizing instruction?

Do we have the answer for that one!

First of all, you have to believe and help others to understand that the learning going on in a classroom is more important than the teaching. Regular use of lots of skills activity centers designed to promote increased understanding and effective use of basic skills in meaningful settings will help to convince the "back to basics" crowd that good, sound individualized educational experiences can actually be used to help a student move *ahead* to mastery of basic skills. Such a skills activity center should present one or more specific, well-defined basic skills with provision for personal prescriptive practice and strong reinforcement of each skill through written or oral evaluation techniques. (For a plain English translation of the above and an easy-to-follow guide for implementation, see SPECIAL KIDS' STUFF by Farnette, Forte and Loss.)

I've been using free-choice interest centers for years—I think! Exactly what is your definition of a free-choice center? Is there a new and better way to use such a center, and can you offer ideas to heighten interest and give pizzazz to this age-old idea?

Read on!!

Playboys, pleasure-wanderers, traffic jams and weary

travelers are simply inherent in some individualized classrooms. How does one deal with the kinds of problems related to kids not being able to employ themselves constructively, avoid overcrowding at major centers of activity or interest and eliminate the fatigue and frustration that often threaten such a busy, activity-saturated climate? The establishment of free-choice interest centers or "open" centers can absorb a major portion of these kinds of problems. These are centers which are open to any student at any time, are not assigned or prescribed and remain virtually stationary for a longer block of time than do most centers —though the experiences and resources they offer may change often. We like to think of them as the "life-learning" stations—non-subject-oriented oases from the pressures of the more academic centers, but complementary to the so-called content areas.

The purpose of the "open" center is to stimulate imagination and creativity, provide opportunity for the development of thought processes and problem-solving techniques, set the stage for original contributions in product development and stimulate fast-maturing concepts of self-worth and facility in self-direction and discovery. Here, a child may get to know himself better, find the niches where he is most comfortable and learn in what areas he is most able to make valuable contributions.

Looking For Something To Do???

—A simple poster-like list of suggestions for the

early-bird, the weary or the wanderer. Includes odd jobs around the classroom, items to be researched in the dictionary or encyclopedia, suggested projects, helping younger students, preparing materials, relaying messages, adding to the library, changing a center or bulletin board, assisting the teacher in some manner. Include surprise items (i.e., "On the page opposite the word 'aardvark' in the dictionary, find a special 'special privilege' coupon!).

Minute Station

—Potpourri of activities which can be completed in one minute or less. (When a student completes one, he must replace it with a suggestion of his own.) Supply timer or stop-watch.

Brain Busters

—A constantly changing and expanding collection of brain teasers and puzzles for fun, relaxation, information and mental exercise. Make it attractive—use come-on gimmicks and prizes. Set time limits. Ask kids to contribute.

Tinker Trunk or Patent Office

—A trunk full of gadgets, tools and junk to be "tinkered" with, taken apart, made into new things, etc., by the younger set.

Older students like the dignity of the patent idea. (You might send for real applications to the US Patent Office.) A list of suggestions to spark ideas might be helpful.

Invent: something to make a classroom job easier

something to use as an aid to memory

something unique on which to build a learning center

a device to "beat" a system

something to use as an instrument of measure, etc.

The Think Tank

—A long, sturdy piece of cardboard rolled into cylindrical shape (or any substitute which provides a small, enclosed one-man space). Suggestions which spark creative and productive thought should be written graffiti-style on the inside walls.

Sound Center

—Tapes and records with a variety of stories, songs, ideas for "jumping off" toward some area of experiment or study. Books, scripts and/or pictures accompany some recordings. Others are for listening only. Some include follow-up activities. Add instruments for experimenting with sound and rhythm ideas and records for interpretive dance.

Don't neglect to include teacher-made tapes of stories, ideas, etc., on which are also interspersed some special personal messages to one, several or all students who use the center.

Rabbit Hutch

—It's an add-to kind of center where you supply the basic ingredients and the kids make it happen by expanding the idea. A simple example would be to present a mobile on which hangs one large-sized noun. Supply clothespins on which kids write every conceivable adjective describing the noun, and attach them to the mobile without destroying its balance!

Similar activities may be effected with drop-boxes, balloons on sticks, add-on animals, bulletin boards, etc., using a variety of content-related symbols, such as prefixes and suffixes, parts of speech, titles, derivatives, synonyms, number combinations, etc.

Readers' Room

—Most important ingredient: comfort! (Use rugs, pillows, an old mattress, rocking chairs. Let the kids furnish it.)

Second most important ingredient: gobs of fascinating reading materials to cover many interests and levels.

daily newspapers
catalogs
advertising pieces

manuals
cross-word puzzles
cereal boxes
travel brochures
atlases, maps
comic books
pamphlets
magazines (include: *Hot Rod, Popular Mechanics,* movie magazines, etc.)

The Teacher

What is the role of the teacher?

An important one! As children become more familiar with the learning center approach to classroom instruction, the teacher's role becomes increasingly less overt. The teacher moves from lecturer, instruction-giver and chief evaluator to become the true facilitator of learning.

The planning that precedes the establishment of a learning center, the provisions for meaningful use of relevant materials, the clear and concise instructions for center activities and the established criteria for continuous self-evaluation free the teacher to break out of the lockstep pattern of the teacher-dominated classroom. In this manner, the teacher's approach can shift to meaningful academic counseling and the role potential immediately becomes more creatively exciting for both students and teachers.

Does the teacher have more free time?

Yes. . . . more time free to encourage learning! Once the learning center is operational, students should be able to proceed at their own rate in completion of the learning tasks and in employing and recording results of the self-checking activities that accompany them. Thus the teacher will be freed of routine instructions, grading, and general record-keeping. This precious "free" time can be well used to work with students on an individual tutorial basis or with a small group

59

exhibiting homogenous needs. Children are especially responsive to "having the teacher all to themselves" or to the exciting projects that can be attempted by a small group working (or playing) with the teacher's full attention.

If you misinterpreted this question and thought it meant more free time to spend in the teacher's lounge or more nights free from diagnosing students' progress and preparing materials for the next day's use, the answer has to be *no*. No one has ever proposed learning centers as leisure for the lazy or rest for the weary.

What happens to substitute teachers?

They may have a rough day! On the other hand, the total involvement of an open classroom is contagious, and the substitute teacher just might "catch" the excitement and become "hooked" on it. Some substitute teachers give testimony to the insights they have gained due to their experiences in classrooms using learning centers, while others bemoan the sad state of "modern education" and contemplate looking for other outlets for their professional energies.

The most desirable approach to solving this problem is the addition of a brief orientation session for substitute teachers to the initial teacher training program. Three or four days of directed work with an additional two or three days devoted to an internship arrangement should be adequate. If the budget does not allow for luxuries of this nature (as most of them probably will not) substitute teachers interested in working in open space classrooms might be required to simply spend a full day acting as a teacher aid in a selected center.

One advantage of the learning center approach for substitute teachers is the student motivation that results from personal involvement. Their desire to continue with projects underway and the independence acquired from self-directed behavior will enable them to pursue current interests with less teacher guidance. Students in a learning center setting are also much better equipped to "pass along operational procedures" to the substitute teacher. The careful pre-planning for center development is a big help in this regard.

The substitute teacher willing to approach a learning center classroom with flexibility and an open mind should have few problems. If, on the other hand, his tolerance for freedom of movement and pupil spontaneity is low, he may be in for a difficult time. (One might say, the swinging substitute teacher will have his chance to swing, but the non-swingers need to ask for other assignments.)

Will children continue to look to the teacher as a model?

The teacher of young human beings is always a V.I.P.! The model role is a very important component of teacher influence in the open school setting. The free-

dom afforded children to observe, monitor, make value
judgments and reject or accept teachers' behavior as
worthy of their adoption make it mandatory for teachers to consider carefully their approach to classroom
relationships, cultural exchanges and personality
traits. Maintaining the fine line of interdependence
that children must have to give them the security and
reinforcement needed to experiment and try new approaches to learning, and at the same time, inspiring
the desire for independence and self-direction so essential to individualized instruction is a big order.
Realizing the significance of the model role, teachers
moving into a learning center setting need to assess
their degree of mastery in the areas listed below. (If
refinement in some areas is in order, then priorities
leading to improvement should be established and
realistically worked toward.)

- Flexibility
- Sense of humor
- Organizational skills
- Communication skills
- Rapport with parents
- Open-mindedness
- Acceptance of differences in students
- Openness to constructive criticism
- Energy
- Enthusiasm for life

- Intellectual curiosity
- Sensitivity to human needs
- Overt aesthetic appreciation
- Emotional stability
- Objectivity toward self and the profession
- Manner of speaking
- Quality of observation

How does a teacher make the "big change"?

Not very easily! Decades of experience have burned "teacher" upon our mental imagery as that tallest, loudest, strongest, most dominant figure in the classroom. And we seldom picture that figure anywhere but *front and center*. With that kind of indelible reinforcement, the person for whom the role change becomes most difficult is the teacher himself.

The best this "graven image" can do is look at himself as he is—then as he wants to be—and begin to effect a plan whereby he exchanges the old characteristics for the new. Try tackling the project this way:

Make a list of single characteristics that describe the "teacher" you are now.

Example:

1. direction-giver
2. teller (talker-at-people)
3. disciplinarian

Now make a list of characteristics which describe the "teacher" you idealize.

Example:

1. personal consultant
2. resource guide
3. confidant
4. tutor

Can you think of some specific ways in which you might begin to move from thinking and behaving in terms of "class" and "group" toward thinking and behaving in terms of "individual" or "person"? List them.

Example:

1. Develop a life-prescription to meet at least one human (not academic) need of each child in my class.

Name	Need	Prescription
John	loses temper easily	Use "note-in-pocket" technique.
Nancy	"flighty" — never finishes projects	Team with Sharon (a student with strong self-motivation) and give personal attention to project on colonial dolls.

Doug	poor self-concept	Use "job-application" strategy with personal conferences.
Pam	cries when she doesn't get top recognition	Use *Values To Live By* — Arnspiger, Steck-Vaughn Co. 1967 as a model for a story about a girl like herself.

(As the "teacher" image has etched itself upon the decades, so has the job description— "reading, writing, and arithmetic." Thus we are preparing auditors, authors, and journalists—but what about people? If John "blows his stack" everytime someone touches his desk in passing, how will he respond to the pressures of an office manager, a drill sergeant, or a nagging wife? If Pam can't bear to be anything but Number One in her fifth grade class, how can she emotionally handle the promotion of the secretary at the next desk or a simple neglect on the part of her husband to compliment her evening meal? The bank can help her balance that checkbook in 30 minutes, but it may take hours of counseling and years of tormenting emotional upheaval to make living a happy experience for Pam, the young housewife. Is there something you can do to pave the way for the Johns and Pams in your classroom? That's the prescription!)

2. Develop an interest-oriented independent study for each student. (It may take eight weeks to gather information and get everyone "in orbit," but when you can capitalize upon the personal interests already alive in the learner, the learning thrives. If his passion be rock music, boats, horses, karate or hair-styling, make the best of it. There are few interests that can't be used as a base for exploring math, social studies, science, art,— the whole gamut of content and skills.)

3. Build more personalized parent relationships. (You the teacher are to expedite parent-child relationships, not to become the third party of a triangle affair. Anything you can do to enhance the parent-child relationship improves the child's chance of growing up as a happy, healthy, human being.
Experienced teachers find that the "early offensive strategy" works better with parents than the later "report-card time defensive moves." Teachers who are highly successful with parent relationships recommend keeping parents informed by some means of weekly or bi-weekly communication. Letters, conferences, "trial" report cards or anecdotal

calendars kept by both parties and shared periodically are just a few of the ways this can be accomplished.)

 NOTES: An outline form for guidance in self-analysis and future planning toward CHANGING TEACHER ROLE is available in the appendix, Part III.

For further information, see **How will parents react to learning centers?** Chapter VI.

Can any teacher use learning centers?

Let's talk about that! In order to function effectively as a facilitator of learning in a learning center setting a teacher will need to:

(1) Be committed to belief in the worth and dignity of human beings, each entitled to his own unique individuality.

(2) Be more concerned with the learning taking place in the classroom than with the teaching.

(3) Be capable of creating and maintaining an environment for learning that is creatively flexible.

(4) Be able to tailor both methods and materials to meet varying student needs and abilities.

(5) Be sensitive to the rate of student progress and to the need for immediate and specific rein-

forcement as the "cap-stone" to project completion.

(6) Make time and energy commitments required for consistent evaluation and revision of center activities as necessary to sustain the highest level of student enthusiasm and involvement.

All this is to say . . . not *all* teachers *can* do it! What one teaches in a classroom is what he *is!*

—not what he knows

—not what he believes

—not the philosophies, methods and techniques that have been imposed upon or mastered by him

—not even how well he is able to communicate

RATHER, what he teaches is *deeply rooted* in his image of *himself.*

Individualization is not really a process. It's a way of thinking about learners and learning. Many good teachers are simply not committed to the "openness" and shift of emphasis from formalized group instruction that is necessary for implementation of any individualized program. The question is not, "Can any teacher set up and program materials for learning centers?" but "Can any teacher carry the program out happily and profitably?"

Many teachers give lip service to individualized instruction and continue to "teach" from a base of artificial goals developed to "cover" the group as a whole. Only the teacher who can create, and then live and thrive in the kind of creative, self-directive environment necessary to foster the truly individual or personalized approach to learning, will function most effectively in the learning center setting.

NOTE: For assistance in specific personal evaluation, see the appendix, Part IV: TAKE A LOOK AT YOURSELF!

The Learner

What happens when children move from conventional classrooms to learning centers?

They'll probably have a ball!

Even though a move to learning centers may be a bit confusing at first, most "learning center" teachers of the authors' acquaintance feel that few children have difficulty adjusting to the new environment. At first, some children may tend to take advantage of the freedom afforded; others may be over-stimulated and try to do too many things at once, sacrificing quality for quantity. Shy or less secure children may be confused and uncomfortable about narrowing choices, getting started or assuming responsibility for following through to project completion without constant teacher direction.

The time necessary for adjustment to the new environment will be an individual matter and will, of course, be determined by each child's past experiences, emotional set and general adjustment potential.

The wise teacher will make provision for giving students both the time and help needed to launch out on their own for the first time. Assuming responsibility for their own learning is a wonderful opportunity, but one that not all students are prepared to receive graciously.

Teachers will need to make every effort to see that centers are carefully explained to students and that they fully understand what is expected of them. When a transfer student comes into the new setting, the assignment of a "buddy" who will be responsible for him during the first few days may be of great comfort.

How can the needs of each learner be determined?

Take measurements! Make appointments for fittings! Find his size(s).

He's only one whole person, but his feet don't measure the same size as his neck or his waist, and no part may be the size measured last spring. Herein lies the complex task of determining exactly what size he is *now* in each area and then tailoring the teaching to fit his learning needs. Multiply this by the number of learners, and your task is well-defined. You're exhausted already??

Take a deep breath! There must be a thousand ways to tackle the problem. And that adds to the perplexity. Where does one begin? Standardized tests? Cumulative folders? Teacher-made tests? Conferences? Observations? Anecdotal records? Interest inventories? Letters of recommendation (from the pupils, of course)? Sociograms? Personal dialogue?

Try this! Choose three—three *kinds* of measurement that will give you a good idea of personal capability and preference. Don't rely totally on any *one* device, and be sure *at least one* evaluates the student as a person—aside from his academic level of accomplishment.

A representative plan may be to use one kind of

standardized test which would give assistance in some pretty clear-cut determinations about level of ability in the major skills areas. Being mindful that no test is conclusive evidence, however, try to make its result worth no more than one-third of your persuasion about the individual.

A second step would be to devise, on your own, a *battery of short teacher-made tests*—at least one in each major area—that would include items ranging from readiness levels to way beyond what you could expect a child at his present grade level to have achieved. Be sure that children understand the scope of the test and its intent as a mere indication of "size." For example, a test in the math area might begin with matching sets of items or writing numerals, move through simple problems in computation and go on to require operations involving decimals, fractions, story problems and more complex numerical operations. Children must understand that they are not expected to be able to do all problems and that no grade or other indication of success or failure will be made.

A further and more interesting step would be to ask children to make up a second test *they* would use to evaluate understanding of the math concepts they think they ought to be familiar with. (You might even use some of their items on another test—OR make this assignment first and plan to use their tests to devise yours.)

In reading, some provision may have to be made for oral reading evaluation in order to get a sensitive "feel" of the student's confidence and self-concept in this area. Tape recording may be a time-saving technique to use concurrent with teacher-pupil conference.

The third measurement is one which moves away from academic evaluation and makes an effort to provide information on a *personal feeling, interest preference* level. One example of this type of effort might be an open-ended questionnaire or series of statements entitled "ABOUT ME."

Example:

My name is _____

I live _____

I am happiest when _____

You should see our _____

My mother _____

School is never _____

I just love _____

I get angry when _____

When I am alone _____

Students may complete such statements honestly or with intent to be silly, clever or non-committal. Even their choice of treatment reveals something about them. Of course, they are encouraged to answer honestly, but they must know that any information, real or imaginary, will be held in strictest confidence. Neither will they be asked to discuss or defend it in any way unless they choose to initiate such a conversation on their own.

As a further matter of interest and as an indication of good faith on the teacher's part, space may be left on the questionnaire where the student may ask two or three questions of the teacher OR compose several open statements for the teacher to complete as information to the student.

Of course, there is no *one best way* of making diagnoses and placing learners in programs of study and instruction. But it is a little frightening to realize that, for at least a year, a single classroom teacher in effect holds the destiny of the major portion of a child's living. It's even more frightening if that classroom teacher happens to be YOU!

You cannot do more than the best that your skills and understandings will allow, but what is important is that you allow yourself the time and freedom to do what you know to do, and that is to treat each learner personally and sensitively, and open to him as many opportunities for living and learning as you possibly can in the short time that you will spend together.

NOTE: Samples of teacher-made tests and open-end questionnaires may be found in the appendix, Part V: MEASURES FOR PERSONAL DIAGNOSIS.

Why involve students in planning?

It certainly does complicate matters! But the practice is inherent in the whole philosophy of individualization —and to a great degree, the motivation for and success of the process depends upon the facility with which responsibility for learning is shifted from the shoulders of the teacher to those of the learner.

In plain language—if 30 students are going to be involved in 30 different experiences at the same time, either they must assume at least partial responsibility for themselves, or the teacher must be 30 people.

Is there a way to teach students to plan?

Let's take it in three careful steps! Begin by making a *short* list of the *kinds of decisions* that you feel can be made easily by your students *now*.

The list might appear similar to this:

1. Keep daily attendance records.

2. Determine the number of students to be accommodated at each center.

3. Plan for the arrangement of writing materials at centers.

Next, make a list of responsibilities that can be absorbed more gradually and note a suggestion as to how each might be accomplished. For instance:

WHAT?		HOW?
1. Keeping records of daily progress.	1.	• Teacher • Dependable student • One "check-point Charlie" (student) appointed to keep record for each center • Each individual recording his own
2. Setting up one center.	2.	• Appoint committee —ask each child to contribute one item (i.e., suggestion, question, picture, etc.). • Committee organizes information, materials, evaluative measures, etc. with teacher guidance.
3. Choosing student guide or resource for each center.	3.	• Teacher leads group in determining duties of a guide and setting up criteria for choosing a guide. Students decide how selection will be made.

Note: As progress is made toward these goals, you will want to keep adding to this list until "the shift" is effected.

Now, keeping in mind what changes you feel can be made immediately, and the progress that can be effected gradually—make as complete a list as possible of your *ultimate* goals and objectives.

Example:
1. Students determine criteria for grading and methods of reporting to parents.
2. Students conceive *many* and set up *most* centers.
3. Students are fully responsible for operation of centers.

NOTE: A suggested outline for the above procedure is available for applied use in the appendix, Part VI: SHIFTING RESPONSIBILITY TO THE LEARNER

Are there less formal ways to prepare students for becoming involved in their own planning and evaluation?

Try introducing them to personal goal setting! Even pre-schoolers are capable of achieving this at quite a sophisticated level!

Begin by asking each student each day to specify one academic goal (something he promises himself he will accomplish in his school work) and one personal goal (something he wants to do about himself). Encourage them to keep goals very simple—i.e. 'I want to learn to spell *Tennessee*' or 'I am not going to say the word *ain't* even one time today.' 'I am going to learn my 5's multiplication facts.' 'I am going to keep my desk clean.' 'I am going to smile at least five times.' 'I am going to say one nice thing to dumb old Mr. Jones.' As students become more proficient, their goals may become more complex or greater in number.

Reinforce the goal-setting process by specifying a time early in the day during a class *buzz-session* for determining, and if possible, writing down the daily goals. At the end of the day's *buzz-session,* ask students to reconsider their goals and evaluate their achievements. Ask some students who are comfortable doing so to share their goals and self-evaluations as examples so that members can learn from each other how to deal with success and failure.

Personal conference times are good times for talking with individuals about goal-setting. Help them to be realistic in setting attainable goals but goals that present challenge, and help them to understand their own successes and failures in achieving goals.

How do you keep track of *who's where when?*

You've got to have a system! It doesn't have to be complex or fancy. And it doesn't have to be ledger perfect. It only has to suit the situation and give the teacher as much security as he needs to account for the whereabouts of daily activity.

Most teachers will feel at ease if a simple outline or list can be made available to each student, stating exactly what tasks he is expected to accomplish during a given time period (hour, day, week, two-weeks, etc.). The student then becomes responsible for checking off each item as it is completed and reporting his progress in the required manner.

Assignments may be made in the form of checklists, prescriptions, schedules, time-tables, etc., and may be as plain as a type-written sheet of paper or as creative as a party invitation. They may be designed for daily or long-term use, and may be prepared totally by the teacher, by the student himself or as a cooperative effort. The important concerns are that the student know exactly what course to follow and that the teacher be able to tell at a glance exactly what tasks have been completed.

Perhaps the most expedient method of offering ideas and suggestions for developing a successful system for "tracking" is to present examples taken from the files, folders, desks, and bulletin boards of live, creative classrooms where learning centers are in operation. Special note may be made that all of the exemplary systems offer some element of choice and alternative assignments, and many classrooms maintain a permanent arrangement of open or always-available centers which change from time to time in their focus of interest. These open centers may be visited at any time by any student. They not only provide variety, spice and added freedom to the entire

program, but act as buffers or safety-valves for traffic
snarls, communication hang-ups, rainy-day droops and
taut tempers!

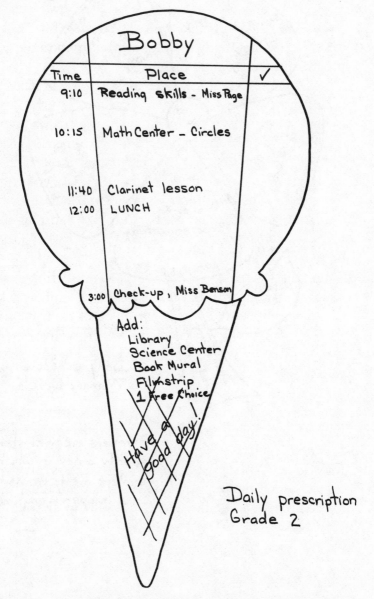

Time	Place	✓
9:10	Reading skills - Miss Page	
10:15	Math Center - Circles	
11:40	Clarinet lesson	
12:00	LUNCH	
3:00	Check-up, Miss Benson	

Bobby

Add:
Library
Science Center
Book Mural
Filmstrip
1 Free Choice

Have a
good day!

Daily prescription
Grade 2

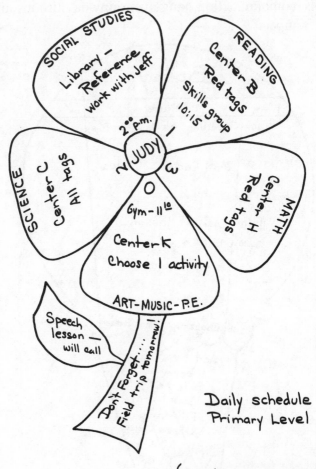

Daily schedule
Primary Level

(numbers near center
specify order in which
centers are to be visited
— O is "open" — anytime)

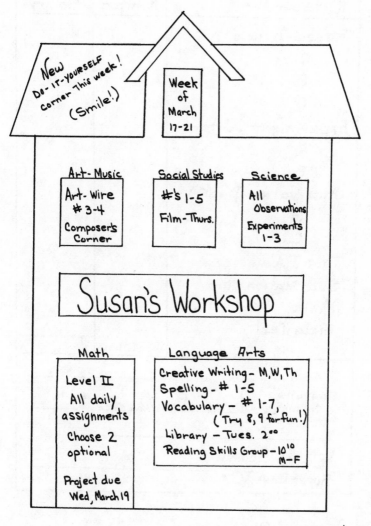

New
Do-it-yourself
corner this week!
(Smile!)

Week
of
March
17-21

Art-Music
Art-Wire
#3-4
Composer's
Corner

Social Studies
#'s 1-5
Film-Thurs.

Science
All
Observations
Experiments
1-3

Susan's Workshop

Math
Level II
All daily
assignments
Choose 2
optional

Project due
Wed, March 19

Language Arts
Creative Writing - M, W, Th
Spelling - # 1-5
Vocabulary - # 1-7,
        (Try 8, 9 for fun!)
Library - Tues. 2⁰⁰
Reading Skills Group - 10¹⁰
                    M-F

One-week prescription
Level 3-4

October—16 - 27	Monitor	Salary
Research Lab		$
C		
F		
G		
Experiment Center		
A		
B		
Observation Deck		
B		
C		
"Test Tube"		
"Sub-station Zero"		
Movie		
Field Test		
	TOTAL	$

_____ 19____

Pay to the
Order of _Dana Buchanan_ $____

_____

V CALLEY Science _____
C REST
SUPER BANK V

Science Classroom
Two-week Assignment
  Level 5—6
(Each activity carries monetary value)

How much should students have to say about evaluation and grading?

A lot! After all, it is they who are being evaluated and graded.

If you can, in your imagination, recreate the feelings of anxiety that were yours as a college freshman facing the first battery of examinations and pending grade points. You voiced your concerns in questions such as, "Over what material will we be tested?" "What kind of test will it be?" "Will it be graded 'on the curve'?" "For what percentage of my grade does this test count?"

Do you really expect that your fourth graders feel any less apprehensive about their "day of reckoning"?

What you can do to involve students in decisions about evaluation and grading may depend somewhat upon your school's philosophy surrounding such matters. Whatever the accepted pattern, and however it is viewed in terms of your own philosophy, there are many ways in which students can participate in determining meaningful guidelines for evaluating their own learning and still guarantee that the end results will meet standard school practices.

Be honest with students. Discuss the grading system—its advantages and its disadvantages. Let them decide what indications of success and failure will best help them achieve their goals. Talk with them about "failure"—why and how it happens, and what can be done to undermine its existence and right its degrading effects.

Below are just a few suggestions that may serve as sparks or starting blocks for such conversations.

- Let students do their own grade reports.

- Let students fill in grade cards the first week and use as pace-setters or goals for achievement. Re-evaluate every Friday; change reports if desirable.

- Make a basic decision as to whether a final grade will be a composite score, an average of all grades or whether it will be an indication of progress made.

- Ask students to recommend a new grading system to improve upon the existing one—and perhaps a way in which the two may be meshed so that they may co-exist if necessary.

- Give a grade in every subject every day.

- Change from grades to "points" or "pay-scales" (Of course, then you have to deal with job-opportunity, job-equality, etc.)

- Ask students to keep *anecdotal calendars* of progress in each subject. The teacher keeps one also for each child. Periodically, they compare their records and make cooperative decisions about progress.

- Ask students to write a letter to themselves stating

"goals for the week" each Monday. Seal and mail on Thursday to the pupil's home. Over the weekend he may evaluate his accomplishments (perhaps sharing his evaluation with his parents) and bring a self-progress report to school on Monday. (There is room for many variations on this one!)

- Teacher and pupil confer to fill in grade cards the first week of each grading period, put them in the drawer and forget about them—just work to learn.

- Prepare narrative report that can be shared in a three-way conference with student, teacher, and parents. The report may or may not be prepared in teacher-pupil conference. It may be used alone or concurrent with grade reports.

- Do away with grades and reports. Schedule conferences when needed.

What about "cheating"?

It will happen! And that's a promise—presuming you define cheating as "copying" or "using someone else's head or paper to get the answers filled in on your paper."

In the open, independent atmosphere of a learning center setting, how does the teacher cope with a cheating problem without destroying the whole thrust and purpose of her program?

Listed below are some strategies for dealing with the cheating problem and their corresponding, projected results. The purpose of this list is not to suggest alternatives but to provoke thoughtful, sensitive treatment of such practices on an individual basis.

Response to cheating

1. "Cheating is cheating!" Call it loud and clear— label it sin.

2. Discovery is met with amazement — "I can't believe you'd do such a thing!"

3. Minimize public attraction. C a l l a private conference with the offender(s).

Result

1. It g o e s underground. (Harder to detect.)

2. A punctured ego, at least. Practice probably continues with greater feelings of guilt.

3. Depends entirely upon t h e rapport between conferees and the resulting real personal commitments. At best, the student emerges feeling the teacher is really "rooting for him" and sees the cheating as a deterrent to his own personal goals; thus he proceeds with renewed positive determination and no guilt feelings.

At worst, the student emerges embarrassed—perhaps belligerent or apathetic—and nursing an already negative self-concept.

4. Ignore it!

4. That which arises as the result of a "lazy-day" or "easy-dollar" attitude is l i k e l y to disappear. That which is the result of real anxiety remains.

5. Pretend to ignore it, but privately analyze and seek to negate causes.

5. Hopefully, t h e symptoms disappear as the antibodies take over.

6. Encourage it!

6. Some child might learn something "copying" that he would never have learned on his own!

7. Require it! (Design carefully)

7. Students may learn to work cooperatively. If you pair w e a k and s t r o n g students, the weaker usually benefit; older w e a k students with younger students, both benefit; two weak

students, a leader emerges and at least one, if not both, benefit. Bargain exchange—he does work one day, his p a r t n e r the next— neither will let the other become a leech; each will become the other's h a r d e s t taskmaster. Thus, both profit.

What about discipline?

Well, what about it? Nobody *we* know has ever proposed to have the final answer to this question!

Learning centers work best for teachers and students who have already had a "meeting of the minds" and have subscribed to a preventive rather than a corrective approach to the problem.

Rules for classroom living that are developed "by" the group "for" the group seem to work well. An absence of "thou shalt nots" and an abundance of "thou shalts" designed to promote peace and harmony within the group, and at the same time afford the maximum freedom of movement for individuals is highly desirable.

The framework for this set of pupil and teacher-prepared guidelines will need to make provision for the increased movement and heightened noise and activity levels which are by-products of learning centers in use. Increased utilization of both materials and space impose new pressures on the classroom. These pressures make it even more important for teachers to plan carefully as they test ways of sharing, taking turns and paying respect to the rights of others. (This includes the right to privacy which is sometimes very difficult to come by.) Children want and need the security that comes from well-defined limits within which to operate.

Even with the most carefully developed plans and the optimum teacher commitment to a positive approach to discipline, some children will continue to have more difficulty than others in acclimating to group living. Whenever possible, behavior unacceptable or disturbing to the group should be redirected rather than censured. Fortunately, this is a relatively simple matter when several learning centers are operative within the classroom. Presenting a child with alternate activities often serves to free him from the unproductivity of a negatively reinforcing situation.

Teachers who look at behavior discrepancies within their group as challenges rather than threats have taken the first giant step toward establishing a creatively democratic classroom environment.

It is this kind of environment that encourages boys and girls to develop trust and respect for fellow students and for their role as responsible members of the society in which they live. One very perceptive teacher we know says, "I never have a discipline problem. I only have planning problems."

NOTE: For further insights into the teacher's role as related to classroom control, read **Where can I buy an insurance policy for peaceful living during the "transition"?**
—Chapter VI.

Will all students profit from working in learning centers?

No one approach to learning is best for all children. While individualized instruction is highly desirable for all students, it would be unrealistic to assume that the learning center approach would be the panacea to work this miracle. Most students will be motivated by the opportunity to make free choices related to their learning. Some children may, however, be lacking in the independence and self-direction necessary to make good progress in this approach to instruction.

Then what shall I do with those students who "can't, won't or don't"?

Plan something different for them.

The problem of the unmotivated student has been with us always. Individualized programs based on

student interests and personal involvement have low-
ered the incidence of students lacking self-direction
considerably, but have not eliminated the problem.
These students require special planning and handling
in any organizational design.

Again, it is of the utmost importance for teachers
to know and understand these students as individuals
and plan for them on that basis. More teacher-
directed activities of a structural nature may be in
order. If so, they will need to be planned to operate
concurrently, and yet not interfere with the learning
centers in use by other students.

Can you be more specific . . . p . . p . . please!!

*Sure—that's what's so great about an individualized
or learning center approach. . . .*

It provides a latitude in day-to-day, hour-to-hour
operations that no other approach can offer. At the
one extreme, a student or group of students may be
involved in highly structured activities where and when
they need or want them; simultaneously, it allows for
almost unlimited freedom in learning styles for another
group of students.

You want to be specific—let's cite some alternative
techniques and strategies for dealing with learners who
need special attention.

1. *Grounding:* This strategy may be imposed by the
   student himself or suggested by the teacher and

agreed upon by the student for one of several reasons. Some students get just plain "antsy" in a bustling, activity-oriented classroom. They need a hide-out, some peace and quiet away from the madding crowd. They might ask, "Please, may I have a desk of my own in a quiet corner with some ordinary old written assignments and a pile of text books?" Heavens, yes!! Provide for it! Decide together how you can create a "private office" or corner for this person. He or she just needs a break! Another student might be what would normally be labeled a trouble-maker, or at best, "a distracting influence—a traveler." This person may need grounding simply to get his own head in order, settle himself down, practice setting attainable short-term goals and working toward them carefully with guidance or close supervision. He or she may need to work toward a pre-determined "reward goal" of free time or of time back in the mainstream of activity just a few short periods each day until he feels able to handle constructively his own prescriptive activity. For some students, "grounding" may be a one-day respite from the thundering herd. For others it may be a 3-month ordeal of working carefully and methodically toward developing self-discipline. It should seldom, if ever, be used purely as a punitive device. Rather, it needs to be a strategy, acceptable to both teacher and student, for achievement of a very important personal goal.

2. *Sabbatical Leave:* Unheard of? You thought sabbatical leaves were granted only to university professors. Well, what better solution can you offer the highly capable student who has developed a deep and compelling interest in a biological science-related project? Why not grant him leave from the usual prescriptive program to arrange study time in the library, the museum, the high school biology lab, etc. Work with him to develop a personalized program of study in his field of intense interest which integrates the math, social science and language arts skills and concepts which he needs with his scientific research project.

3. *Independent Study:* This technique may be used simultaneously and in conjunction with the regular center-focused approach, or as a separate supplementary activity. Many teachers have found that independent study projects are most effective and rewarding when students are required to fill out application forms stating their purposes, their plan of operation and a statement of their goals and probable resources before they embark upon such a venture. The application is then discussed in a personal conference with the teacher, and plans are well-defined and confirmed.

4. *"Open" or Free Choice Interest Centers:* A rather general but perfect answer to the special needs of nearly every individual learner at one time or another. (For complete information, see Chapter 2.)

5. *Mini-Centers:* Mini-sized, high-interest, highly personalized, self-directive, portable, one-person, multi-disciplinary and mighty—and with lots of other good characteristics for the "itinerant," the "restless," the "self-stimulated high achiever," the "handicapped," the "home-in-bed-for-a-week," the "non-motivated," the "accelerated," the "under-achiever" and all those youngsters who find it difficult to fit into the mainstream of classroom activity. (This solution is more completely defined in Chapter 2.)

6. *Highly-structured Prescriptive Activity:* Especially for students who seem unable to determine attainable and challenging self-goals or who have difficulty pacing themselves in efficient use of time. This technique is also appropriate on a short-term basis for those who need intensive care in the development of a specific skill operation—either an academic or personal life need. It should be employed only upon mutual agreement between teacher and pupil with a specific time goal for re-evaluation of its worth.

With whatever strategy or technique one might choose to handle special kinds of problems or problem learners in any classroom setting, there is one paramount consideration to be kept in mind: we can teach and drill and practice with kids until they can write perfect sentences, speak with clarity, express with dignity, compute with accuracy and read with fluency, but our job is not to turn out authors, orators, lecturers, journalists, copy-readers and bookkeepers. Our purpose as educators is to facilitate the development of human beings—fathers and mothers, husbands and wives, friends, employers and employees, executives, implementors, leaders, followers—PEOPLE who desperately want to and have to communicate with one another in order to survive. Does it not shake your very being to the roots to realize the awesome responsibility that lies upon the shoulders of the classroom teacher? Choosing the appropriate alternative technique for helping a student to learn a set of number facts may have a remarkable and permanent effect on his development as a human being. How important it is to make wise choices!

What happens to children who move from learning centers to conventionally organized classrooms?

They will probably be frustrated, but not permanently damaged! Most children who have become accustomed to the freedom of movement and the challenge that comes from personal involvement in learning will resent a move back to a more traditional approach in instruction. This resentment may manifest itself initially in the form of hostility or lack of motivation for achievement. Here again, the degree of frustration and the time necessary for adjustment to the new situation will vary with individual children and their flexibility and ability to "find their way." An additional factor may be the quality of the learning center situation from which the move is made. (A few children may welcome the familiar structure of the traditional classroom.)

Many champions of open education argue that any experience enabling children to assume responsibility for their own learning is better than none. They feel that the self-direction and motivation for personal achievement that the child enjoys for even a limited time will help him to direct his energies and efforts more constructively in any future situation.

Certainly the threat of a move backward does not provide a good reason for the conscientious teacher or administrator to forestall a move toward innovative procedures offering increased opportunities for students. It may well be that students moving from schools with learning centers to conventional ones may serve as catalysts in promoting the spread of the learning center approach to individualizing instruction.

How can learning centers be used to channel physically handicapped, academically disabled and other special students into the mainstream of classroom learning?

We don't have a magic wand, and we can't offer you a magic formula, but we do propose that the learning center approach to classroom instruction can provide a certain degree of "mainstreaming magic." Since the very heart of learning center planning focuses on goals and activities designed to provide for individual differences in learning abilities, learning rates and learning styles, the mainstreaming objectives are established at the planning level rather than at the implementation level. More specifically, several approaches encompassing student options can be easily provided for every single learning center. Students with widely varying ability levels can work effectively and harmoniously within the same learning center setting and with the same skills or concept goals *when* the pre-planning, instructions and materials preparation have been based on concise and consistently up-dated knowledge of individual student needs, interests and abilities.

This kind of learning center planning can and should replace the old, fixed three-group approach to instruction. A real bonus, too, is the flexibility afforded: a student may move naturally from one center level to another with little trauma. Additional incentive for broader student interaction and improved self-concept is made possible since a given student may be working at one level in reading, another in math and still another in creative arts.

 NOTE: For specific examples of three learning center plans encompassing learning goals and strategies to meet varying student abilities, see Chapter 2.

How is the child's self image affected?

He can grow and grow, and still be himself!

We know children learn in different *ways* and at different *rates*. Oftentimes, however, we are at a loss as to how to provide multiple activities to better meet these individual needs. Teachers with strong commitments toward honoring differences in children continue to be puzzled as to how to go about creating an environment rich enough in materials and experiences to accomplish this miracle.

Well planned learning centers, presenting activities with goals and procedural expectancies planned on the basis of individual differences, may be one answer. As children work through center activities, they experience the satisfaction that comes from selective involvement in projects meaningful to them at the time. In addition to this, the increased opportunity to associate more freely with members of their peer group and learn from "others doing" as well as from "doing" is a fantastic boost to the child's developing self-confidence.

Nothing breeds success like success! As children

complete center activities that are realistically planned for their developmental readiness stage, they move confidently toward the next achievement level.

Will this kind of freedom encourage children to be self-centered and "too individualistic"?

It shouldn't. Actually, the constructive self-satisfying experiences afforded by good learning centers help children develop the security prerequisite to concern for other people. As they move from center to center, selecting materials, using the library and drawing on other resources, students will have ample opportunity for interaction with members of their peer group. Courtesy and respect for the rights and privileges of others will be called for on an individual as well as a group basis. It should be remembered too that the use of learning centers does not eliminate group activity. Groups are organized for specific purposes and are disbanded or rearranged as these purposes are accomplished and new ones arise.

I'd like to know my students better, but I find that difficult to do during the busy school day. Could you give me some suggestions?

Try these!
   —Each time you have recess duty, make it a point to spend part of that time with one student.
   —Keep a communication box (i.e., the MAILBOX

or a **BACK TALK BOARD**) available at all times—a place where the students may say anything to you at *any* time.

—Drop in on special after-school activities to which individuals belong in order to see them in a non-classroom setting (i.e., clubs, intramural sports, etc.). Also, when possible, try to attend a special dance or piano recital, Little League ball game, etc.

—Write lots of personal notes—the letters you get in return will tell you all kinds of things about your students!

—Give a personal call or visit to sick students.

—Let each kid be V.I.P. for a day. Provide time and space for him/her to share or show important and special things.

—Invite individuals to stay inside to help you at recess time or after school.

—Have the students create "Who Am I" collages in which each individual creates (from magazine words and pictures) a collage about himself and superimposes the ideas on a silhouette of his profile. (You do one, too!)

—Use lots of casual interest inventories.

—Give each student a chance to plan a special surprise for the day.

... A SPECIAL LOOK AT THE
VERY YOUNG LEARNER ...

What are the advantages of learning centers for young children?

Freedom to be themselves! The curriculum can be implemented in a more flexible manner in order to take into account individual differences in children's interests, abilities and past experiences. We know that young children today accumulate many bits and pieces of information from widely varying sources. We know too that the pre-school program must be designed to help them sort out and gain meaningful use of these unorganized and unclarified concepts. The learning center approach can provide the freedom of movement needed for children to experiment, to question and to deal with their own intellectual curiosity in their own way, at their own rate.

Carefully planned opportunities for observing, experimenting, talking and listening will serve to widen horizons. Children can be encouraged to develop inquiring minds, sharpen their in-born curiosity and extend their awareness of people and events in the world through direct experiences that are relevant to their personal development stage. Through the center activities, differences in background and experience as well as differences in physical, emotional and intellectual needs can be dealt with.

Academic disciplines (social studies, math, language, etc.) can be subtly dealt with in order to provide as much exposure as children are ready to cope with and yet not become overwhelming or result in undue pressure for achievement.

Experiences in the appreciative areas such as music, art, creative drama and literature can be made much more meaningful when they are presented through individualized "fun type" projects which eliminate the pressure for peer group approval and rigid performance standards.

Don't young children need the security of a closely defined space and one teacher?

Four walls and a warm body do not necessarily equal security! For too long we have labored under the misconception that a "closed" environment afforded young children a feeling of security. At no developmental stage in the life span is freedom to experiment and explore the total environment more important. This is not to infer that young children need to be thrown into a chaotic environment without the guidance of concerned, knowledgeable adults. They are, however, much more adaptable to the stimulation of open-space education than many teachers and parents

think. The environment can so easily be structured
to promote early education through the discovery approach.

It is important to maintain the feel of continuity
from one day to the next and to encourage children's
sense of security through exposure to "known" adults.
If team teaching is to be part of the learning center
program, teachers who have had no prior experience
as a member of a teaching team need to take every pre-
caution necessary to function effectively. Some time
spent in studying and planning together *before* the
actual center work begins is a must.

Both teachers and children need to be clearly aware
of who is responsible to whom for what. Good clear
guidelines for space restrictions and project initiation
also serve as "security blankets" for both teachers and
students. These guidelines need to be realistic, simple,
firm (but not rigid) and easy to understand. Remember, they will be the tie that binds.

What are some examples of centers for kinder- garten and first grade?

Try these for starters, but your own list will be better!
The teaching-learning process for young children is
so very personal in nature, each teacher and group
of students will most likely find their center demands
and interests unique to their own situation. This list
is intended to be merely suggestive of basic areas that
lend themselves readily to center development.

Social studies and/or language centers can be designed to provide language development, exposure to socio-cultural concepts and mastery of skills needed to gain additional information.

Some examples with suggested equipment are:

1. Housekeeping Center
   playhouse furniture
   dolls, bed, and carriage
   utensils
   dress-up clothes
   large mirror
   movable screens

2. Geography Center
   simple maps and globes
   compass
   charts, chart holder
   drawing materials
   chalkboard
   bulletin board
   sand table
   table and chairs

3. Reading Center
   bookshelves, magazine rack
   rug
   rocking chair (s)
   pillows

books
magazines
bulletin boards, peg boards
reading table
chairs
word cards

4. Listening Center
round table and chairs
tape recorder and/or record player
tapes and/or records
several sets of earphones (6-8)
peg board
chart, chart tablet

5. Safety Center
table and chairs
bulletin board
chalkboard
many signs
charts, chart holder
books

6. Writing Center
table and chairs
bulletin board
chalkboard
shallow storage shelves
chart, chart holder
writing materials
picture dictionaries

7. Oral Language/Dramatics Center
chairs
multi-purpose puppet theatre, puppets
tape recorder and/or record player
tapes and/or records
trunk of old clothes
books

8. Holiday Center (seasonal)
bulletin board
table and chairs
shelves
books and manipulative materials

9. Self-Awareness Center
full-length mirror
paper
pencils, crayons
books
masks
hats

Art and/or music centers can be designed to provide for experiences in creative expression and aesthetic appreciation. Some examples with suggested basic
equipment are:

1. Painting Center
easels
plastic sheets or mats to protect floors
paint
brushes

paper
tables
drying lines or racks
sponges for cleanup
smocks or aprons

2. Clay Center
large round table
clay keeper
clay

3. Construction Center
soft wood
nails
hammers
screws, screwdrivers, bolts, nuts
vise
glue or paste
cardboard
scissors, string
cardboard
tacks

4. Drawing Center
crayons, box paint
paper
scissors
paste
charcoal, chalk
pencils
bulletin board for displaying work

5. Appreciation Center (Music and Art)
   filmstrip projector, filmstrips
   record player and/or tape player
   records and/or tapes
   bulletin board
   shelves
   table, chairs
   chart, chart holder

6. Listening Center
   record player and/or tape player
   earphones (6-8 sets)
   sing-along records and tapes
   records introducing orchestral instruments

7. Instrument Center
   large picture cards of orchestral instruments
   guitar
   ukelele
   horn
   recorder
   drum
   full set of rhythm instruments

Math and/or science centers can be designed to make provision for development of number concepts and awareness of scientific methods and marvels. Some examples with suggested basic equipment are:

1. Observation Center
   live animals, plants
   table and chairs

      aquarium and filter
      terrarium
      incubator
      ant colony
      thermometer
      shelves
      animal, insect cages

2. Experiment Center
      large bowl(s)
      clear plastic glasses
      hot plate
      storage shelves
      heat-proof glass dish
      air pump
      five hand lenses
      chart, chart holder
      bulletin board
      chalkboard
      table and chairs

3. Counting Center
      table and chairs
      abacus, one large and 6-8 small
      blocks, several sets of varied sizes
      beads and strings
      peg boards and pegs
      flannel board and flannel objects
      large number cards (both words and numerals)
      bulletin board
      chart, chart holder

4. Problem Center
   table and chairs
   chart, chart holder
   chalkboard
   (any items from Counting Center may be borrowed)

5. Store Center
   multi-purpose store frame with shelves and a variety of "saleable" items
   play money
   toy cash register

But how do children who can't read know what to do?

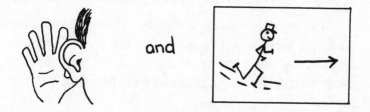

By using good listening habits and a super-set of hieroglyphics!

Not more than 2000 years ago, man's communication with man depended heavily on gestures, pictures and primitive forms of graffiti. And his messages were probably as well understood as ours which now are so totally dependent upon the written word.

The teacher of very young children or children whose mastery of reading skills is yet undeveloped enjoys the challenge of communication at this primitive, natal stage.

Fortunately, today's teacher has at his disposal a modern world of highly developed knowledge and technical aid which can be used to great advantage in "getting the message across."

He doesn't need expensive or fancy equipment, but he can use a full store of personal ingenuity. He will find himself counting heavily on the development of good observation techniques, listening skills, and manipulative interests and abilities in his students.

His live voice (or a recorded substitute) will be a major asset if he has learned to be precise and succinct. (Giving oral direction is, in itself, an art.)

He needs to teach his students how to observe, using all their senses to gain information. Then step-by-step, by concrete example, he must lead them to carry that knowledge gained to its practical application.

He may rely on high-interest manipulative-type tasks as a way of assigning independent activity and as a way of evaluating on a non-verbal basis, the understanding of concepts taught.

Most importantly, he will make every effort to keep his methods of communication and the tasks required of his students on a level relevant to their world, familiar to their language patterns, ethnic setting and social practice, and he will seek to make every moment of their learning highly useful to them in their daily lives.

The following pages present a few examples of ways information may be provided to or extracted from children who have limited reading skills.

Making Pudding

1. Put pudding mix into bowl.

2. Fill cup with milk.

3. Add milk to mix in bowl.

4. Stir mix a long time with the spoon.

5. Pour pudding into dishes.

Pet Center

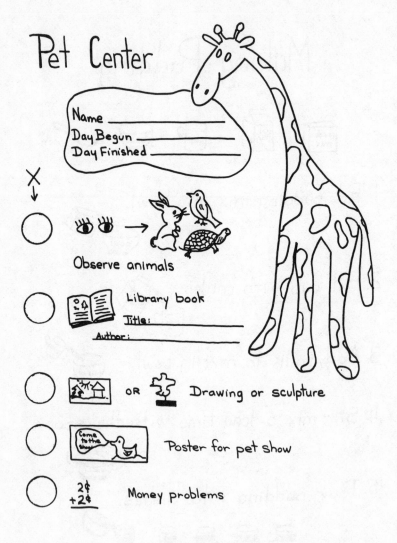

Name _____
Day Begun _____
Day Finished _____

○ Observe animals

○ Library book
Title: _____
Author: _____

○ OR Drawing or sculpture

○ Poster for pet show

○ $\frac{2¢}{+2¢}$ Money problems

Pet Center

Name _____
Day Begun _____
Day Finished _____

☑ as you complete activity

☐ Observe animals , do ?'s

☐ Library book
  Title _____
  Author _____
  Comment _____
  _____

☐ Drawing or sculpture

☐ Ad for pet show

☐ Money problems

Did you enjoy being clerk at the pet shop?

A POTPOURRI OF IDEAS

For Working With Young Learners

... Sharpen motor skills and awareness of size and weight by allowing children to load and unload shelves full of canned goods, stacking small on large, arranging by size, shape, weight, color, classification of foods, etc.

... For climbing and for dramatic play, a kitchen stool or short step ladder can easily be made into a "tree house" or "bridge" or "cave" by taping paper props to one or more sides.

... Make thumb puppets for children by using washable felt-tips pens to draw faces on thumb nails and add hair, hats, etc. on the thumbs.

... Children love to touch and hold small animals, but often the animals tend to get away. Seat the child in an empty vinyl wading pool while he plays so that both child and animal are safe.

... Create a stuffed animal farm or "petting zoo" made up of the children's own stuffed animals. Attach to each animal a label card or tag bearing its name. On a wall or cabinet nearby, place larger tags bearing the same names. Ask children to match the tags and say the names of the animals until they have learned by rote to read each name. Then detach the tags from the animals and see if children can match the larger tags with the appropriate animals.

. . . Young children are natural cleaners and scrubbers! Provide squeeze and spray bottles full of water, paper towels or clean cloths and special "work" times for cleaning windows, sinks or shelving units.

. . . Let children paint the outside of the building, playground equipment, your car . . . with brushes and water!

. . . To avert the late-afternoon "cranks," take a walk or play a stretching body-movement game to relax everyone.

. . . Encourage a child to make a "book train" by laying end to end every book he has read or had read to him. He may then walk or crawl along beside the line and tell the name of each book or what each is about and identify his favorites. "WOW! See how much you know about books already." What great reinforcement!

. . . Keep a big box of cookie cutters which children may use to draw around, make shape pictures and practice cutting skills. Great for motor coordination.

. . . Pouring water is great fun for preschoolers, and provides lots of opportunities for learning about volume, weight, capacity, etc. Children may sit around a vinyl swim pool or large dishpan or washtub, or one child may sit in one side of a double sink and play in the other. Be sure to provide lots of sizes and shapes of containers for pouring.

... Need quick, easy cover-ups for painting and pasting? Cut a head hole in the center of a double-fold newspaper sheet and slip it over the child's head. It may be tied at the waist for more secure protection.

... BOXES . . . BOXES . . . BOXES . . . to sit in, hide in, climb in, play in, paint, build towers, trains, buildings, stack to fall . . . a million uses. Be sure always to have some on hand!

... Cans with plastic lids make much better "crayon keepers" than the traditional boxes. Also, the newer cone-shaped crayons provide more durability, less breakage, more coloring surface, and are easier to hold and more fun to use than the straight traditional crayons.

... Give a child a pile of pillows. He'll think of lots of things to do with them!

... When you really want a child's close attention, whisper and roll your eyes as you speak!

... To provide incentive for writing, require that it be done with washable, colored felt-tip pens instead of pencils.

... Sometimes a young child needs just a good, quiet therapeutic activity. Cutting strips or paper scraps from old newspapers is perfect for this. Kids love to do it, and the results can be used later for papier maché, stuffing, packing, etc.

. . . Get them used to measuring in feet. Make a foot pattern exactly 12 inches long and use it to measure nearly every large object in sight. (Use the length of the child's body to measure larger distances. . . . How many Judy's does it take to make a driveway? How many Dave's long is our room?)

. . . ALWAYS provide a quiet place for a child who needs time alone. Call it "A Place to Be" or "The Thinking Place."

. . . Ask your librarian to help you locate books that help children relate to special traumatic situations such as death, birth of a sibling, divorce, illness, etc. Read these to the child, and encourage him to express his thoughts on the subject.

. . . Take photographs of your children fighting, arguing, sad, frustrated, etc.—then loving, laughing, enjoying, etc. Let them compare the two sets of pictures of themselves and talk about their feelings.

. . . Provide a good collection of action and story records and headsets in a place where children may listen and record privately.

. . . Maintain two or three open centers with manipulative materials where a child may experiment with personal ideas, concepts and emotions (i.e. a young child who has difficulty sitting still might find solace in filling small plastic jars with rice or beans and pouring beans from jar to jar . . .).

. . . Good learning centers for young children do not have to be based on reading, writing and arithmetic. Centers can focus on self-awareness, puzzles, creative dramatics, nutrition, grooming, mix & match, motor development, etc.

. . . Write personal notes to the child often!

. . . Hang a full-length mirror in the classroom and encourage children to look at themselves and recognize their own distinguishing features. Develop pride in the person that they are—unique, not like any other.

. . . Each child might have his very own GIANT BUSY BOOK if you can secure enough old wallpaper books. What a treasure for cutting, pasting, drawing, etc.

. . . Paste a different pair of paper ears on each child. Let each pretend to be a real or fanciful animal, choose a name and a role for himself. Sounds like fun!

. . . Making cardboard or paper bracelets is a good way to reinforce words, numbers, names, colors that need to be learned. "Belly Budgers" serve the same purpose: these are merely pieces of bright colored paper pinned to the belly which remind the child of a color, number name or word that needs to become part of his learning. If he wears the symbol all day and has to say the information over and over, he can hardly forget it!

. . . "Clip-King" or "Clip-Queen" for a day is an honor bestowed upon the child who can say the number or letter on each clip-type clothespin. Pins may be clipped or attached to his collar, hem, side of a pant leg, etc. as he identifies each symbol.

. . . Provide a set of eight or ten colorful pictures of children. Ask each child to identify the picture which looks most like himself and tell why.

. . . A large board of locks and keys, latches, hooks, bolts, hinges, etc. is a must in a preschool classroom for experimentation, eye-hand coordination and visual perception.

. . . Always provide a "Curiosity Corner" or a "Tinker Trunk" full of gadgets and fascinating objects to be explored by young hands and minds.

. . . Place a balancing beam in a prominent place in the room. A taped stripe on the floor may be substituted to walk on, jump over, slide beside, etc.

. . . Have a place for everything and insist that everything always be returned to its rightful place. This readiness for orderliness is necessary for more formal schooling and creates pleasant living conditions, both present and future. (Parents and future spouses will thank you!)

... Have an abundance of growing things which may be explored, discovered, analyzed and cared for by the children.

... Ask your young students to help you develop a unique system of signs and symbols just for your classroom—sort of a tailor-made rebus code for the most common centers, activities or items on the daily schedule. Use these in making assignments or referring to duties and responsibilities.

... Some teachers find it very effective to use a short song or melody to denote time for a change in activity. When it's time for lunch or recess, the teacher simply begins singing the familiar tune softly, and the children all join in as they become aware. They all continue to sing or hum along softly until everyone has quietly made the transition and is ready for the new activity.

... Institute a "color" day during which everything is done by colors. (i.e. "If you are wearing a red feather, you may have first choice at the block center." "Blues may have first choice at the animal center, etc.) Use a similar procedure for a "numbers" day, "big words" day, "shapes" day, etc.

... Huge floor-size puzzles (as large as 5 x 7 ft.) made of styrofoam or ¼″ plywood or even heavy chipboard or corregated board make marvelous instructional devices. One teacher we know has several puzzles made of light colors of formica veneer on which she may draw or write various things and then erase them for reuse. She often gives each child a separate piece as he enters the classroom and asks him to place it. Sometimes the finished puzzle will contain a message from her to the class.

. . . Create a color-mix center where there are squeeze bottles of food coloring (the primary colors), water, containers and "recipes" for make the secondary colors.

. . . Tin cans with varying numbers and sizes of holes punched in the closed end or in the sides are great for both sand and water play.

. . . With the use of a polaroid camera, a unique and very personalized first primer can be developed for each individual child. Pictures may be mounted on manilla paper and short sentences written beneath. An indefinite number of pages may be added until each child has assembled a primer of his very own. The story or stories are about him . . . a guarantee they will be read over and over.

. . . Use large, colorful, cut-out letters to greet a different child each morning. Consider how special John will feel if when he enters the room tomorrow morning, he sees a large sign that says, "Hello John!"

... Put a silly message or a joke or a funny picture in an envelope. Place this envelope in a larger envelope, then in a larger one and a larger one. ...

... Keep a surprise box or a treasure chest chock-full of small items that can be used as incentive rewards for various purposes. (Be sure every child gets to choose one now and then.) The box might contain wrapped items such as: candy, a new pencil, a small toy, pencil sharpener, a tiny book, a poster, a bookmark, a ring, a felt-tip pen. ...

... Scraps of wood from the lumberyard, hammers and nails are a must for at least one center of activity in a preschool room.

... An especially intriguing activity center for the younger set can be created with all kinds of "sophisticated machinery" usually associated with the adult world—i.e. a typewriter, record player, CB radio, adding machine, calculator, cash register, telephone, etc.

... Create a play rug with a million uses by appliquéing on a sturdy piece of muslin or kettle cloth various kinds of material cut to resemble roads, farms, airports, parking spaces, gas stations, rivers, lakes, bridges, etc.

... Provide several flashlights which may be used to "write" letters and numbers on ceilings, walls or dark chalkboards—and for making shadow pictures.

. . . Young children love using cameras, binoculars, microscopes and magnifying glasses!

. . . One of the favorite activities of every preschooler we know is that of playing waiter or waitress. Creating a restaurant corner supplied with paper cups and plates, plastic utensils, order pads, pencils, aprons, hats and simulated foods or pictures of foods will provide good practice in following directions, writing numbers and letters, using a coding system. . . and good manners!

Creating the Environment

Does the term "open space" always mean learning centers are being used?

No, not always!

The term open space simply refers to the architectural style of the plant and is not necessarily descriptive of the program taking place inside. More and more lovely new schools are being planned and built to afford the large open areas that lend themselves to innovative curriculum designs. Each school program is dependent, however, upon the philosophy of the adults responsible for its implementation. One often finds the large open areas partitioned off by bookcases or screens to provide the setting for very traditional, teacher-dominated, self-contained classrooms. On the other hand, it is not unusual to find learning centers being used very effectively in old buildings with no provision for large space utilization. It is important to remember too that other methods for individualizing instruction may be implemented in buildings featuring the open space concept.

NOTE: For further information see Chapter II—**Is the learning center design the only way to individualize instruction?**

Do learning center programs really work in old buildings with no open spaces?

It takes some doing, but it is being accomplished every day!

133

Fortunately, the quality of instruction and the commitment to creative teaching and learning has never been dependent on the style or age of the building. Some of the very earliest individualized programs featuring the learning center approach were housed in older buildings with few, if any, modern features. The essential ingredient here is creative teachers, capable of exercising the vision necessary to reorder the furnishings, activities and "school life-style" of both themselves and their students.

Won't I need lots of expensive new materials to set up learning centers?

Not necessarily. The challenge is to use the same old materials in new and exciting ways!

Naturally all teachers long for the excitement and stimulation of lovely new materials. Naturally, too, the availability of a wealth of these materials would help the teacher moving into the learning center approach to provide students with more alternatives and increased motivation for using the center. No expensive materials will do the job of individualization, however. The most elaborate and best-developed materials will continue to be dependent on the use made of them in the teaching situation. Materials and supplies already on hand can be reprogrammed with a minimum amount of effort to offer continuous student progress on an individualized basis.

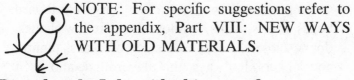

NOTE: For specific suggestions refer to the appendix, Part VIII: NEW WAYS WITH OLD MATERIALS.

But what do I do with this room?

Use every nook, cranny and corner of it!

The importance of the classroom environment cannot be overemphasized. Children are influenced either positively or negatively by their surroundings. A cheerful, well-lighted, comfortably ventilated classroom encourages "good feelings" about school and consequently, the development of a healthy emotional set toward learning. The dullest, drabbest classroom can look brighter and enjoy a new image with a minimum expenditure of money and a maximum amount of creative effort. Before you immediately rule out your classroom as hopeless, let's discuss some basic ideas for using space and materials to the best advantage.

First of all, take stock of what you have to work with. Adequate space to allow for a free traffic flow from one center to another and for creative movement and exploration is a big plus. If space is extremely limited, the effective arrangement of furniture and equipment becomes very important. Space may be logically conserved in "sitting/writing" areas where it is of less value than in areas where activity or relaxed reading will take place.

Rugs and pillows, bookcases, large cardboard
boxes, easels, walls, window sills, window shades,
doors, closets, backs and sides of desks, pianos,
and lockers, hallways, the playground, and even
the ceiling may be ultilized as space for learning.
(If you haven't tried suspending a colorful three
dimensional center from the ceiling, you have a
delightful treat in store.) Corners become very
important when they are used for "quiet corners,"
"choosing corners," "writing corners" or even
"dreaming corners."

Every inch of classroom space can be used to a
good advantage if care is exercised in the overall
arrangement and consideration is given to the
curriculum demands.

NOTE: See appendix, Part X: CREATE-
A-CORNER and Part IX: USING UN-
USUAL SPACES AND PLACES.

Would a checklist for arrangement of space and equipment be helpful?

Try this one for size!

1. The passwords are CLEAN, NEAT and AT-
TRACTIVE.

2. Avoid clutter.

3. Provide some "quiet" areas and some "noisy"
ones. Plan the distance between to facilitate the
optimum use of both.

4. Ventilation and light must be adequate at all times.

5. Color and cheerfulness are essential ingredients.

6. Seating arrangements should be comfortable.

7. Table or desk heights should be adjusted to meet physical needs.

8. Traffic patterns should be "tested" on the basis of the total day's activities.

9. Provision should be made for both small group and individual work.

10. Provision should be made for completed work to display clearly and attractively.

Will housekeeping be more complicated?

Not if you plan ahead! As is true in a home, an office building, or any other physical setting for the activities of more than one person, the classroom that allows more freedom of movement for more people will be subject to more wear and tear. This does not necessarily mean more clutter, disorder or untidiness. If provision is made for efficient use of materials and for their easy distribution from one area to the other, and for adequate storage of supplies and equipment, many problems can be avoided. All storage areas should be easily accessible and should be clearly marked to enable children to make optimum use of materials with the least amount of teacher direction.

Specific plans for putting things away at the end of a work period should be incorporated into every planning session, and all children should be encouraged to share responsibility for "clean-up" time.

Can students assist in implementing center activities?

Does a teacher need a right hand?

Yes, a student may be chosen to be the keeper or curator of a given learning center. He may be chosen because he is the most knowledgeable about the topic around which the center is created or because he is very naive about that subject. He may even be the person most likely to destroy the center.

His job description includes the following:

1. Assist in creating and setting up the center.
2. Be able to answer any questions about the use of the center. (Students must ask the center keeper before they may ask the teacher!)
3. Keep materials replenished and in order.
4. Be in charge of a record of center visitors and transfer this information to the teacher's master chart.
5. Check work done at the center (optional).
6. Assist in dismantling and storing the center.

> NOTE: The center keeper should not be required to stay at his center all day. He

should be free to move about his business as any other student, simply checking back at the specific center in between each of his daily activities.

Are there some specific precautions to take before centers are introduced?

Yes, it's better to be safe than sorry!

1. Be sure to check plans for completing and evaluating the center activities *before* they are presented to the children.

2. Present the directions clearly and in detail. Break them down to the simplest level so that they will be understood by *all* the students.

3. If directions are written, exercise caution in printing and arrangement. Use large, neat type.

4. Check to be sure all supporting materials such as books, pictures, worksheets, filmstrips, records, tapes, recorders, etc. are easily available.

5. If materials such as pencils, paper, crayons, etc. are required for an activity, place them in containers at that center rather than asking children to supply their own. (This saves much confusion and "travel" time for retrieval of forgotten materials.)

6. Plan for "traffic flow" in relation to other activities that will be taking place while the center is in use.

7. Look forward with enthusiasm to a new and exciting experience in trying a "different" approach to teaching and learning.

Exactly what steps need to be taken to prepare students to begin work in a given learning center?

That's a very good question! Probably one of the most pertinent you could ask.

In order to be clearly definitive and specific, let's list items that need to be considered in introducing a group of students or any individual to a given center, task, project or unit of study.

1. ALWAYS point out the location and name or number of the center. Identify the character and major content of each assignment.

2. Give specific instructions for attacking the required tasks (what to do first, second, third, etc.). The less able student needs the most direct and detailed directions. If necessary, ask students to repeat or re-explain the instructions to check their understanding of the assignment.

3. Be sure students know what materials are included in the center, how to use them and how to care for them.

4. Give students a probable timetable for completion of the center.

5. Leave no doubts as to what is expected in terms of performance or achievement at each center, and be sure students understand how this will be evaluated.

6. Last, but very important in terms of efficient operational procedure, give students a checkpoint where they may review the above information or get help, should they forget or misunderstand initial instructions. (This may be provided in writing or by a knowledgeable student helper, center keeper or aid. Make the teacher a *last* resort!!)

P.S. Not incidentally, provide some opportunity for student evaluation of the assigned task—his personal and subjective assessment of its value to him and its appropriateness to his learning needs.

Making the Transition

How do I get started?

Slowly and cautiously!

It is important for children to feel comfortable about moving from any familiar organizational plan to a new and unknown one. The move to learning centers should be gradual, and should encompass familiar practices as well as new patterns to afford students time to experiment and to "find their way" without undue pressure. In most instances it will be wise to set up only one learning center in the beginning and give instructions for its use very carefully. Even though the temptation is strong to "convert" instantly to learning centers, it pays to move slowly and cautiously and to involve the students in every phase of classroom reordering and center development.

Clear and concise directions for use of the centers will facilitate their introduction and initial use. Directions that can be followed with the least possible input from the teacher are highly desirable. New centers should be added gradually in order to avoid the sense of frustration that could result from over-stimulation caused by the preparation of too much independent activity at one time.

But what do I actually *do* to begin?

Anything! . . . that helps you move from where you now are toward where you want to be. Panic won't work. Taking a calm, honest inventory of your assets and liabilities—both personal and professional—then an objective survey of the circumstances and resources which make up your environment will give you a reasonable R.Q.—"Readiness Quotient." That's your clue for where to begin.

What *can* you do—first, easily, with your maturity of teaching skills and sensitivity—then with a bit more effort, courage, preparation, and perhaps moral support—and finally with some bonafide blood, sweat and tears?????

Here are some ways other teachers of varying R.Q. have begun. Perhaps the suggestions will be helpful.

1. *Full-scale Master Plan*—(R.Q. = "Super-teacher") This strategy is not to be confused with "taking over"—i.e., away from all student involvement. Rather, it is a careful, logical over-all plan of attack. Presumably it will take many hours of thought, list-making and elaborate blueprints for arrangement of time, space and materials.

   A certain amount of this is inherent in any good plan of operation, but preparing for the metamorphosis of a total program is quite some ordeal. It presumes a careful diagnosis of and provision for the needs of all students and entails not only the design for a complete instructional program and the placement of each pupil, but also a careful plan for a total physical environment which is highly complementary to the goals of the curriculum.

Often this method is selected by a school system or a "team" of teachers who wish, all together, at a given time to convert from another teaching-learning concept to the learning center approach.

2. *Choose One Content Area and Expand*—A safer and simpler way to "try your wings." Begin by choosing the subject or content area with which you feel most confident—or which you feel lends itself most readily to the learning center concept. Make careful plans to individualize for just the time which will be spent each day or week in the pursuit of that one subject. When the plan is working smoothly in that subject, expand by individualizing in another subject, then yet another until as much of the curriculum as desired is implemented on this basis.

One caution!—Don't feel pressured into hurrying. Take time to gain confidence and facility with each area before moving to the next.

In all probability, as units of study and classroom climate changes are made, however gradually, there will be temporary set-backs. Take time to "work out the kinks." As simple a matter as the room temperature or the clarity and attractiveness with which instructions are pre-

sented can make all the difference. Try to remain sensitive to real causes and effects. It's
easy to get side-tracked or become discouraged
by difficulties which are only symptomatic—not
real ills.

3. *Choose One Time Period and Expand*—Many
   teachers have found beginning success in setting
   aside one large time block each day—or perhaps
   just several days each week—for the purpose of
   moving toward more personalized teaching.

   For example, a period of 9:15-10:30, Monday through Friday or 2:00-3:15 on Monday,
   Wednesday, and Thursday might be chosen. During these specified hours, students move into
   learning centers or independent study programs
   for work in one or more subject areas.

   Much like the idea of expansion in content
   areas, the individualized approach may then be
   widened to envelope more and more of the
   school day or week until as much of the curriculum as desired is presented on a personalized
   basis.

   This plan has merited particular success where
   teachers have designed to work as a team, and
   students may be moving between several classrooms during the designated time periods.

4. *Grouping, then Paring*—A familiar framework
   on which to build as slowly and carefully as
   anyone may need to proceed.

Most teachers are already at home with "grouping" patterns and procedures, so for them, it is an easier point of departure toward the personalized approach.

Once homogenous ability or skills groups are formed in a given subject area such as math or reading, the process becomes one of paring or shaving each group carefully, setting each individual on his own one-by-one as time and ability to work independently allow. During this intermediate "development" stage, the remaining students continue to work in groups. In ability grouping, it is wise to begin paring either with the most able students (who probably will most quickly gain facility and interest with their new independence) and work toward the middle—OR begin with the least able group (whose needs and academic inadequacies are most evident, or at least easiest to isolate). It is that vast area of middle ground that is most difficult to cultivate. Thus, a bit of practice on either or both sides may be desirable.

A similar pattern may be followed by establishing homogenous *"interest"* groups from which further in-depth interests or ideas may be specified and pursued.

Another point of departure might be to begin with the 5 or 10 students in the class who are *most trustworthy* or *able to work independently*—regardless of their academic prowess—

and move from there toward developing independence and self-responsibility in even the most insecure class member.

Once again quality, not quantity, is of essence. Pare slowly and sensitively, searching out the precise level and place of interest most appropriate for each student.

Patience is the key virtue in this operation. It may take weeks or months to set 36 students in personal "orbit" and insure to the "universe" a calm and peaceful order, but whether it be accomplished at a rate of five-a-day or one-a-week, the rewards in terms of excitement for learning in the classroom will be great.

5. *Team Approach*—Adventure and excitement love company (and insecurity needs and often profits by it.)

For those who want to take the individualized route, but are a bit shaky about "map-reading," a team of traveling companions can be of great comfort and benefit. If two heads are better than one, then a composite of teaching strengths and a rich bank of ideas has to be a winning combination.

For example, a teacher who feels weak in organizational skills may be complemented by the super-manager across the hall, and one who is at loss for new ideas may find encouragement in the fresh outlook of the first-year teacher next door. Sharing the responsibility for everything from the content itself, personal counseling of individual students and the preparation of instructional aids and materials to professional "duties" and the ever on-going generation of ideas, can bring new life and challenge to the whole process of meeting learners' needs creatively and effectively.

Should I explain the rationale for an individualized or personalized instructional program to students? If so, how?

Aren't you more comfortable when you know what's going to happen to you and why?

Level with your students. Let them know that this particular plan of classroom organization has been chosen—not because it is an educator's Utopian dream —not because it is the magical solution to all learning problems—not even because it is guaranteed to meet all individual learning needs. It is simply a more interesting and more personalized way of learning which you believe is more closely related to living.

Paraphrased—it is a chance for each person to be himself—"do his own thing" in the context of a living, working democratic community setting.

However, students must also understand that in order for this approach to work effectively, each member of the learning community must take upon himself

much more responsibility for his own learning and that
of his classmates.

How can I impress upon students a keen sense of the added responsibility which a personalized instructional setting imposes upon each of them?

By refusing to take the responsibility yourself!

When you take away the tradition, the constant
presence of authority, the rules, the restrictions—then
each person becomes a part of a democratic system,
and has a unique responsibility to every other part.

You can't just tell students about it and then expect it to happen. . . . You have to lay careful ground-
work and *live* the concept fully and completely so that,
by your example, they begin to understand it.

It might be initially explained like this:

*A community has leaders and followers, and critics
of leaders and followers. It is made up of conformists
and non-conformists, joiners and loners, infants, children, parents, senior citizens (i.e., people who represent all degrees and stages of maturity in knowledge
about and skills for living), people pursuing different
interests and lifestyles—and yes, people who hold con-
flicting ideas and have opposing patterns of behavior.*

*The contributions made by every one of these peo-
ple are equally important—both in their negative and
positive aspects.*

Our goal is to create a democratic community

*setting which is equally personally rewarding to each
of them.*

Case in point: *In a democracy, it is only in institutions
that people are forced to line up, sit in rows, do the
same thing at the same time.*

*In life, we do these things only when they are
necessary for orderliness or efficiency, or sometimes
for courtesy (such as at ticket booths or lunch counters
or bus stops).*

*Thus—in this real life democratic community we
call our classroom, we don't have a lot of rules or a
dictator or a police force; we simply determine among
ourselves, or more plainly, make an open, honest
verbal commitment; each to all the others, to conduct
ourselves in a polite, orderly and respectful manner.*

*P.S. It must be clearly understood that when one
member violates his commitment he hurts not only
himself but the entire community. (For instance, when
the class must wait one minute for Henry to get his
supplies together, Henry has not wasted one minute,
but one minute times the number of people who are
waiting. He owes the community an apology!)*

Reinforcing this concept of community responsibility may seem restrictive and unnecessarily punitive, but
if the importance of responsibility to the community
is over-emphasized and exaggerated at the first incidence of violation, it will quickly be absorbed by an
overriding respect for others and a determination to
create a happy, relaxed and functioning democracy.

It is the role of the total membership of the community to create an open, honest, caring environment in which this kind of catalytic experience can occur without needless embarrassment to or harrassment of one "errant" community member. The attitude of the leadership in this community makes all the difference —especially at the beginning.

What are some of the pitfalls I should be aware of as I make the transition?

Add your own to this list of eight!

1. *Planning to work with too many children at one time.* Some centers lend themselves to large group activity; others do not. For example, a large group of students might very attentively view a short filmstrip and participate in a brief follow-up discussion, while the very same group of students could certainly *not* participate as a group in finger painting or an instructional math presentation featuring manipulative materials.

2. *Counting on "busy work" to keep students occupied in a learning center while the teacher attends to recordkeeping or other chores.* Students accustomed to the academic stimulation afforded by the open space approach are not apt to be lulled into a false sense of achievement through the use of meaningless activities of the "bead-

stringing" or "worksheet" nature—not for long, anyway.

3. *Failing to give attention to scheduling in order to provide a good balance of quiet and active periods and of structured and free times.* Students need variety in their day but they demand and must have some time to "be themselves" and "to do their own thing."

4. *Approaching the school day without adequate preparation.* Students are the first to know when the center is not "ready," and their tolerance level is low indeed for the teacher who tells them "to be good" while she finishes cutting out the paper dolls they'll be using for their social studies project or runs to the workroom to duplicate worksheets for the math lesson. The rule of the game is "Ready or not, here we come," and it pays to be ready.

5. *Failure to provide open-ended materials and experiences that allow students to move at their own pace and employ their own learning style.* Creativity and discovery are individual in nature and even when students work harmoniously in a group setting, skills are acquired and concepts are gained at different rates and in different ways. Each center *must* make allowances for these differences by providing activities with varying achievement expectations.

6. *Unrealistic timing.* Knowing the attention span of students and planning accordingly is essential to center scheduling. Discipline problems will be natural outgrowths of rushing from center to center or from allowing an experience to drag on beyond its climax.

7. *Lack of specific evaluative criteria.* The importance of evaluation of center learning cannot be overemphasized. Teachers and students need the security that comes only from "measuring" in specific terms both quality and quantity of learning taking place. When objectives for each learning center are concise and specific in nature, evaluation is integrated as a natural part of the activity. Then the joys of discovery and self-motivation are reinforced immeasurably by the satisfaction that is a result of recognizable personal achievement.

8. *Leaving students with "dangling loose ends."* All center activities should be planned for completion in a logical sequential manner with a pre-determined culminating point. In appropriate instances, a finished product such as a worksheet or art project may serve this purpose. If so, students should be given good, clear directions as to what to do with it. Improper attention to details of this nature can result in loss of pride in completion of activities and foster careless organizational procedures.

How can the learning taking place in centers actually be evaluated?

By using proven techniques in new and creative ways!

Evaluation is basic to the creative learning process that learning centers are designed to promote. As teachers and students work together to measure the effectiveness of skills and concepts being acquired, the desired open-ended approach to continuing learning is nourished.

Evaluation ought to be viewed as simply the means through which the teacher and his students can determine what has been learned so that new activities can be planned to build upon and extend this learning.

Gone are the days of broad global objectives that sounded good on paper but had very little application to the actual classroom setting. The learning center approach demands the statement of practical objectives, planned to measure in specific terms the learning taking place in a given center at a particular time. Many teachers are profiting from the use of behavioral objectives developed to include anticipated behavior on the part of the learner, the conditions under which the learner will work to demonstrate the behavior, and the standard of minimum acceptable performance.

The important thing to remember is that even though evaluative devices may be planned and presented to individuals or groups, the results are meaningful for diagnostic and prescriptive purposes only when they can be applied on an individual basis.

Some evaluative devices that can be modified and used effectively and creatively in learning centers are:

- anecdotal records
- manipulative bulletin boards
- open-ended questions
- games or quizzes
- crossword puzzles
- logs and diaries
- teacher-made tests
- student-made tests
- charts and posters
- creative drama
- art projects
- checklists
- tape recordings
- suggestion boxes
- secret messages
- scrapbooks
- dioramas
- building and constructing
- creative writing
- experiments
- records of observation
- charts, graphs and diagrams
- interviews , discussions, debates

Is it important to provide for student evaluation of the individualized program itself?

You bet your life!—and the life of the program!

How else will you really know if it's working for an

individual? That person is the kingpin. It's happening to, for and about him and her—and for their edification.

Ah–but *how* do you make provision for such evaluation?

Listen!

If you're not a natural listener, force yourself! If you've built a very positive, open classroom environment with optimum communication benefits, you'll be getting good, pertinent feedback on a continuing basis. Of course, it's probable that you will always have some talkers—students who are more than willing to give you the benefits of their unsolicited opinions. But if your goal is to understand life-affecting results of this teaching approach for each and every student, you will probably need to create specific opportunities for response to given activities and experiences as well as to the program as a whole. A *back-talk board* where students may ask questions or make anonymous comments may be helpful. Early-morning and end-of-the-day *buzz sessions* which precipitate free, open communication between teacher and students provide another check on the pulse of student reaction. *Private mail box* communication between teacher and individual student (sometimes it's easier and more comfortable for people to "say it in writing") and individual conferences (for face-to-face confrontation) are grand facilitators of evaluative dialogue.

Where can I buy an insurance policy for peaceful living during the "transition"?

On your salary you could hardly afford it—even if such a thing were for sale. Obviously, this kind of "insurance" has to be indigenous to every individual classroom, but there is a skeleton "policy" to which one may subscribe, and the adoption of some security measures will result in greater dividends for the general pleasure and enjoyment of living in your classroom.

The "policy" you develop will necessarily have to do with three basic areas of concern: *personal behavior, use of centers,* and *communications systems.* In the most idyllic situation, these three areas are jealously guarded by an all-encompassing atmosphere of freedom and mutual respect, impenetrable by iron hands, stringent laws and intolerant attitudes. Of course, the elements that make up this kind of setting are largely intangible, but a few specific and very tangible measures can contribute to that ideal.

Personal Behavior - - - - Discipline ? ? ?

Behavior is the totality of what one is or how he acts. Discipline, on the other hand, is what is done to order or control behavior. The effect of the individualized or learning center approach, with its relaxed inhibitions and freedom of choice, conjures up a host of nightmarish expectations and anxieties for many prospective subscribers. Volumes have been written on the subject, and as is true of life itself, there are no magic formulas for perfection.

Then too, what is "acceptable" behavior or "good" discipline is so relative a matter that perhaps it is futile to discuss in terms of children and classrooms; rather, it should be considered only in terms of personal taste and tolerance levels. Whatever the code or standard may be in your situation, let your decisions be governed by a truth basic to all activity dealing with human nature—prevention is always more worthy than correction.

Years of experience in dozens of classrooms have brought many veteran "disciplinarians" to the belief that rather than compiling long lists of rules and regulations by which students must conduct themselves, only one big idea or concept seems to be of paramount importance in order to guarantee the pleasantness of every moment of living in that "closed community"— courtesy.

If you can, refrain from that natural professional-directive bent toward "constraining" or "preaching," and merely share with your students your concern (and theirs) for making living in "this classroom, this year" a happy experience for all. Above all, stress that this sharing is done on equal terms, the pleasure of the teacher being of no greater importance than that of the students.

Granted, the teacher as the servant of the school and community has certain inherent responsibilities for the climate and control of the classroom, and pre-

162   NOOKS, CRANNIES, AND CORNERS

sumably, his appointment is an investment of faith in his superior knowledge and understanding of the nature of the teaching-learning process. But in a truly democratic classroom, that position only gives him the "right" to voice his ideas, concerns and opinions as an *individual member* of the group. Yes, he may hold veto power, but in a reasonable sense; and if the desire is to secure a happy, interdependent, thriving family community, authority will always be tempered with reason, fair concern and a keen sensitivity to its resulting effect upon the personal feelings of every member.

Use of Centers - - - - Ground Rules!

In some classrooms, there is very little need for any permanent understandings about use of centers. Once the operation of centers is explained and becomes a natural part of daily routine, things seem to work smoothly without any special regulations.

In other classrooms, it seems wise to set a few standards of use—or at least let them evolve from needs which become evident as the centers become operative. Such rules may govern the number of people who may visit a given center at the same time—or how materials at centers may be replenished or where additional help or information may be found if directions are not clearly understood, etc. The students themselves are most often the best problem-solvers in these areas, and it will be refreshing as well as informative to watch the democratic process in action as they accept responsibility for the ensurance of the efficiency and effectiveness of their own activity.

Communications Systems

"Openness" and "availability" are probably the keys to efficient communication between teacher and students and between students and students.

Though the group may need to make some decisions about how one of its members may indicate a need to communicate with another (i.e., by raising a hand, by writing a note, by merely approaching him quietly, etc.), there must always be a channel open to the individual whereby he may gain attention if he needs it. Blocking or simply not providing such channels will force "blasting"—better known as "misbehaving" or, at its worst, "yelling" for attention—not very pleasant for the community, but quite an effective way of gaining immediate response!

Conversations with teachers who have been successful in maintaining good communications systems indicate that a system works best when it can be natural and life-like. Courtesy is the only restraint. Teachers are always available unless involved in personal conference or counseling, at which time a student may utilize an alternative channel for letting a need be known—for instance, a short personal note pressed into the teacher's hand or placed on a spindle which will be checked as soon as the teacher is available.

Students may communicate with one another at any time as long as they are aware of their responsibility

for the pleasure of the community, and barring in-
terruption of a member's personal involvement in a
conference or project from which he has indicated he
does not want to be distracted. Often, the class will
conceive a clever device which may be used by any
member to indicate his need for privacy—excepting
emergencies, of course!

 NOTE: For further information regarding
behavior and discipline, see **What about
discipline?**—Chapter IV.

What if the other teachers in my school don't share my conversion experience?

Be a missionary! Moving to any new approach in classroom instruction is not an easy matter. It is even less
easy if you happen not to have the full support of
the rest of your faculty. Teachers not yet ready to
move may be extremely "bothered" by those who are.
Some teachers just very sincerely defend their present
methods of teaching by resisting change of any nature
and will make every effort to prevent it. Fortunately,
the freedom (and responsibility) to teach as one sees
fit is a part of the American teacher's professional
heritage.

If you really believe the learning center approach to
classroom instruction will enable you to better meet
your student's needs, and you want to try it, then by
all means, proceed with haste! Yes, even if you are

the *only* teacher in your school who feels this way.

In this event you will want to temper your haste with a great deal of caution; you will need to plan wisely and carefully so that the activities taking place in your classroom are neither threatening nor disruptive to your co-workers.

The enthusiasm generated by you and your students will not go unnoticed by other teachers and students, and you may be pleasantly surprised at the reactions you get once the program is well launched. The sermon you live may be more meaningful than the sermon you preach.

How will parents react to learning centers?

It depends on how good the teacher is at public relations!

One of the things teachers have going for them in this respect is that parents already see their child as an individual. They have watched him grow and develop from a tiny baby into the "student" he now is, and they know that he has his own learning style. Most parents will be delighted by the thought that *their* child is receiving individual instruction and being allowed to progress at his *own* rate. Their problem will be, "How in the world can my child get his share of the teacher's attention if the same amount of time and effort is required for all the other thirty-six children?"

This is when the alert teacher will need to explain

the total concept to parents and show them exactly how learning centers are established and used. When they understand how pre-planning makes it possible for thirty-seven students to be working on different assignments and/or at different levels of difficulty in the same classroom at the same time, they become less concerned about their child's share of teacher time.

It is important for teachers to remember that they are the school's most vital channel of communication with parents. Teachers who are less than enthusiastic about learning centers (or any other innovative program) will have difficulty convincing parents that it really is an improvement over the familiar, traditional methods. One of the best ways to "sell" parents on any school program is to involve them in it just as much as possible. Many parents have the time and talents to enable them to render real service as aides and resource people or to fill other volunteer roles in the classroom. The ones who do not can certainly be invited to visit for observation purposes, to attend class plays or parties, or just to stop by for a brief chat with the teacher. There is no substitute for parent-teacher communication.

Parent reinforcement is of the utmost importance as children move toward self-directed learning. Independent activities that become truly meaningful to children during the school day will have a great deal more "carry over" to the home situation than traditional homework assignments ever had. Parents who are excited about their children's educational en-

deavors and accomplishments and who are aware of
the school's approach to fostering and nurturing these
efforts can become the teacher's greatest allies and the
school's strongest supporters.

 NOTE: For further information, see **How
does a teacher make the "big change"?**
in Chapter III. See also: **A Model Letter—
For Explaining the Learning Center Approach to Parents,** Appendix—Part XIII.

How are homework assignments made?

By those who know best what is needed—the students!

When learning centers are carefully planned to present materials and activities that are intellectually and
aesthetically stimulating, students resist "turning them
off" at the end of the school day.

The books that they elect to take home because
they can't bear to put them down, the reports that are
carried home to be finished before tomorrow's sharing
time or the math problems that were left unfinished in
order to make time for a nature walk will result in
much more meaningful learning than books read to
fulfill the semester requirement, teacher-assigned reports written to culminate social studies units, or page
ninety-seven in the math textbook (which just happens to contain sixteen long division problems).

Students who are actively involved in planning and
using learning centers and who are enjoying academic
success experiences during the school day will just
naturally begin to plan for some part of the learning

experience to transcend the four walls of their school room.

The traditional unexciting homework assignment, made by the teacher and suffered through by the student (and his parents), will ideally be replaced by the student's own "prescription" for out-of-school activities as determined by his own diagnosis—in keeping with his new found sense of responsibility for his own learning.

Will creativity be affected?

That's what it's all about! If we accept the simple definition of creativity as the daring to do something in a different way—to try a new approach to solving an old problem—to look at the world through eyes wide open to some of the beauties and the possibilities that may have been there but were unnoticed—then we are ready to take the first step toward helping children discover and enjoy their own innate creative potential.

Centers freeing learners to move at their own rate and to accomplish tasks in their own way provide an excellent setting for honoring individual differences as determined by ability interests and past experiences. That's individualization—of the highest order!

Appendix

Appendix

PART ONE

A PLAN FOR DEVELOPING A LEARNING CENTER

   I. Objectives—WHAT do you want to teach?
- A. Central Purpose for the center
- B. Specific Purposes for each level, activity, or content area

  II. Tools and Materials—WITH WHAT will you teach it?

 III. Operational Procedures—HOW will you go about teaching it?
- A. Introduction of center
- B. Directions for use
- C. Well-defined procedures for each activity

 IV. Provision for Evaluation—HOW will you KNOW you have taught?
(may be built in as part of operational procedures)

PART TWO

SIGNS, SYMBOLS, and SECRET CODES
—ways of directing learners to their tasks.

1. *Designed Sequence*—That's merely setting up a center so that tasks are numbered in order of difficulty from easiest to hardest. Students with lesser ability are assigned the lowest numbers, while higher achievers may begin at a much higher number. (Of course, all subject matter does not lend itself to this sort of developmental arrangement.)

2. *Color Codes*—Each achievement or interest level at a center is marked by a different color. All tasks on a given level are marked with the same color. Each student is then assigned a *color* or *combination of colors* which denotes for him the tasks to be done by him at that center. He may do different colors at different centers because he is working at different levels in different subjects. (For instance, he may do tasks marked *green* in math, but in language arts, he may do *red* or *red and green.* His prescription might even read, "Do one-half the green, all the red, and try as much of the yellow as you like.")

3. *"Dangling"*—Dangling is what you do when you don't fit neatly into any group or category. It is much like the last above example in color-coding. It allows for a student to do parts of tasks at dif-

ferent levels—one of the distinct advantages of the learning center approach over traditional grouping. There is spacious accommodation for "danglers."

4. *Somersaults and Pseudonyms*—As contrasted with "dangling," somersaulting is just an easy latitude for rolling back and forth—forward to try one's wings on the next most difficult level; backward to review or practice or to pick up some missed skill or information. Somersaulting ought always to be fair play—AND FURTHERMORE, one may at any time elect to cover his Achilles' heel or shield his soft spots (we all have them) by exercising the privilege of traveling incognito—thus, the pseudonym.

"Individualized" activity does not always connote "private" activity, and the protection one enjoys in operating under a pseudonym may be just what a shy or skittish student needs to be able to survive in this atmosphere. He has only to let the teacher know (by some pre-determined method) *who* he is "today" or "in this subject" or "on this particular paper."

5. *Payroll*—Work comes easier for us all when there's a payday ahead. Some students have difficulty following even short-term prescriptions for a sequence of activity with no immediate tangible reward in sight; so keeping a *payroll* is just one way of providing for that kind of need. Rather than working to accomplish a given number of tasks, the student

works toward a total number of points—or perhaps a reward of dollars and cents (in play money, unless the teacher is very wealthy). Each activity or task is assigned a value. When the student evaluates his work at the end of the day, the evidence is clear in terms of points or dollars and cents. If Monday was a $2 day, he may find incentive in working toward a $5 day on Tuesday or toward a final Friday paycheck of $25.

6. *"Love Letters"*—When you want to give that added "I care about you" touch to individual students, try substituting a personal note or letter for the usual daily or weekly prescription or schedule. Take the opportunity to praise something particularly outstanding or note-worthy; offer a special word of encouragement about some personal concern. Say thank you for a simple act of kindness or compliment a neat paper or a pretty smile. Make a habit of sharing a little bit of your human self with each of your students—lovingly.

PART THREE

CHANGING TEACHER ROLES—

a guide for self-analysis and future planning.

A. Characteristics of "teacher" in present role.

1.	6.
2.	7.
3.	8.
4.	9.
5.	10.

B. Characteristics of "teacher" in desired role.

1.	6.
2.	7.
3.	8.
4.	9.
5.	10.

C. Some things I can do to begin moving in my thinking and behaving *toward* more "personalized" teaching. (OR what can I do to steer my thinking from "group" or "class" activity to each "individual" child?)

1.

2.

3.

4.

5.

PART FOUR

TAKE A LOOK AT YOURSELF!

1—Superior
2—Excellent
3—Good
4—Fair
5—Poor

____ 1. Ability to be honest
(not as opposed to dishonest, but *realistic* about yourself)

____ 2. Curiosity
(Are you easily intrigued by simple, wonderful things?)

____ 3. Sense of Wonder
(Can you find delight in blowing a dandelion, watching an ant hill, making pictures of clouds and such, or does it all pass you by?)

____ 4. Enthusiasm—love of life

____ 5. Belief in children
(Do you see in kids more greatness and potential than in any other resource. . . ?)

_____ 6. Ability to *share* yourself
(in a human, personal sense—How do you do at expressing what is really you?)

_____ 7. Creativity
(You define it. . . .)

_____ 8. Energy
(How do you rate your go-power?)

_____ 9. Challenge
(Does what you are inspire and excite? Do you dare others to achieve?)

_____10. Your intrinsic worth or value to the people you work with. . . .

TOTAL _____

How do you measure up? 10? 20? 50?
Keeping in mind the high subjectivity of such a rating scale, what score in your estimation would designate teachers who could thrive in the optimum personalized environment?

178 NOOKS, CRANNIES, AND CORNERS

HOW AM I DOING?
(A Teacher Self-Evaluation Checklist)

Do I show personal interest in every student regularly?

Do I know the academic needs of each student?

Do I know the personal needs of each student?

Am I enthusiastic and excited about teaching?

Am I comfortable with the "feeling" or atmosphere in my classroom?

Am I sharing myself with my students?

Do I laugh, joke, feel at ease with my students?

Am I contributing to the lives of students and of the people I work with?

Am I keeping records carefully?

Do I communicate often and openly with parents?

Are the students involved in planning, making materials and evaluating?

Am I gaining and sharing new ideas?

Do I use other people to help in the classroom?

Am I happy with my own progress this year?

PART FIVE

MEASURES FOR PERSONAL DIAGNOSIS

- A. Primary Reading Interest Inventory
- B. Intermediate Reading Interest Inventory
- C. Math Diagnosis—Primary Level
- D. Math Diagnosis—Intermediate Level
- E. Indication of Social Sensitivity—Primary Level
- F. Think and Know Inventory—Intermediate Level
- G. About Me—Primary Level
- H. About Myself—Intermediate Level

PRIMARY
READING INTEREST INVENTORY

Name _____

Grade _____

Date _____

1. I like to read about _____.
2. In my free time I like to _____.
3. I like people who _____.

4. My favorite author is _____.

5. When I grow up I want to be _____.

6. I don't like books that _____.

7. I'd like to go _____.

8. My favorite time to read is _____.

9. The thing I like to do most is _____.

10. I like to read aloud to _____.

11. What I want most in the world is _____.

12. I like books with _____ pictures.

13. I wish _____.

14. Reading makes me _____.

INTERMEDIATE
READING INTEREST INVENTORY

Complete the following sentences to express your feelings about reading, about school and about yourself. Don't think about them too long. Just write the first thing that comes to your mind. Remember, there are no right and wrong answers. Complete all the sentences in order.

1. My favorite place to be is _____.

2. My favorite time of day is _____.

3. I really enjoy _____.

4. To me, school is _____.

5. The thing I like best at school is _____.

6. I'd like school better if _____.

7. I wish my teachers _____.

8. My classmates are _____.

9. To me, homework _____.

10. Reading is _____.

11. I like to read about _____.

12. The last book I read _____.

13. The library _____.

14. I'd rather read than _____.

15. When I finish school _____.

16. I want to be _____.

17. People are _____.

18. When I was little _____.

19. I feel proud when _____.

20. Better than anything, I like _____.

21. People think I _____.

22. I don't know how _____.

23. I wish someone would help me _____.

24. Long books _____.

25. Newspapers and magazines _____

26. Social studies _____.

27. I worry about _____.

28. Teachers I like best _____.

29. I wish my parents _____.

30. I wish people wouldn't _____.

31. I wish I hadn't _____.

32. Little kids _____.

33. I look forward to _____.

34. Television is _____.

35. I get angry when _____.

36. I don't understand why _____.

37. Art is _____.

38. Holidays are _____.

39. My favorite T.V. program is _____.

40. Of all the books I've read, my favorite is _____

_____.

41. To be grown up _____.

42. Something that bothers me is _____.

43. I like to _____.

44. If I could do anything I wanted at school _____

_____.

45. Most of all, I wish _____.

MATH DIAGNOSIS–PRIMARY LEVEL

Match the sets and number words with the numerals

△ △ △   4   ten

○ ○ ○ ○   10   four

□ □ □ □ □   3   three

卌 卌   6   six

Find the missing addends.

___3___ n + 4 = 7   _____ n + 0 = 8

_____ n + 3 = 10   _____ n + 3 = 9

_____ n + 4 = 9   _____ n + 5 = 10

_____ n + 1 = 7   _____ n + 4 = 5

Find the differences.   Find the sums.

10 — 6 = n __4__   7 + 3 + 2 = n _____

9 — 5 = n _____   4 + 4 + 0 = n _____

14 — 9 = n _____   3 + 6 + 7 = n _____

12 — 7 = n _____   6 + 7 + 4 + 3 = n _____

11 — 6 = n _____   5 + 7 + 3 + 2 = n _____

Story problems.

1. 11 boys.
   3 went to sleep. How many awake?

2. Caught 16 fish.
   7 got away. How many left?

3. 8 balloons.
   6 hats.
   How many fewer hats than balloons?

4. Had 14 cents. Spent 6, then spent 3.
   How much spent? How much left?

5. 4 red fish
   12 blue fish
   How many fish in all?

6. Ate 3 apples, then 2 pears.
   Ate 3 oranges too.
   How much fruit did I eat?


```
   32        65        72        61        60
  +35       +21       −44       −25       −23
```

```
                                         234
  345       436       6782       123
 +738      +744      +4329      +764
```

$3 \times 2 =$ $6 \times 6 =$ $54 \div 9 =$

$7 \times 8 =$ $2 \times 0 =$ $36 \div 3 =$

$9 \times 7 =$ $8 \times 8 =$ $72 \div 8 =$

$4 \times 4 =$ $7 \times 6 =$ $42 \div 7 =$

$4 \times 7 =$ $9 \times 3 =$ $60 \div 10 =$

$6 \times 5 =$ $8 \times 4 =$ $48 \div 6 =$

$3 \times 5 =$ $5 \times 4 =$ $35 \div 5 =$

$$\begin{array}{r} 54 \\ \times\ 7 \\ \hline \end{array} \qquad \begin{array}{r} 62 \\ \times\ 6 \\ \hline \end{array} \qquad \begin{array}{r} 285 \\ \times\ \ 5 \\ \hline \end{array} \qquad \begin{array}{r} 619 \\ \times\ \ 8 \\ \hline \end{array}$$

$6\overline{)126}$ $5\overline{)325}$ $8\overline{)344}$ $5\overline{)160}$

$$\begin{array}{r} 3657 \\ +4369 \\ \hline \end{array} \qquad\qquad \begin{array}{r} 654 \\ -276 \\ \hline \end{array} \qquad\qquad 7\overline{)448}$$

$$\begin{array}{r} 846 \\ \times 5 \\ \hline \end{array} \qquad \begin{array}{r} 923 \\ -357 \\ \hline \end{array} \qquad 8\overline{)596} \qquad \begin{array}{r} 396 \\ \times 6 \\ \hline \end{array}$$

$$4\overline{)373} \qquad\qquad \begin{array}{r} 396 \\ +936 \\ \hline \end{array} \qquad\qquad 9\overline{)342}$$

Write some problems of your own. Do them.

Match the columns.

circle	1 foot
triangle	2 pints
parallel	$4\overline{)28}$ with 7 above
line segment	24 hours
right angle	2/3 and 4/6
quotient	△
equivalent fractions	═══
1 day	(circle with line)
1 quart	16 ounces
12 inches	
improper fractions	○
inscribed angle	(line segment)
	(right angle)
1 pound	8/5 and 6/6

MATH DIAGNOSIS—INTERMEDIATE LEVEL

7	6	8	6	49
+5	+8	+3	+7	+23

85	38	12	17	15
+73	+19	− 5	− 8	− 9

52	68	84	803	871
−13	−49	−27	−171	−109

$603	72	49	$4276
−387	46	61	5079
	83	46	6213
	51	71	4875

$5\overline{)25}$ $7\overline{)49}$ $8\overline{)48}$ $4\overline{)36}$

87	82	856	483
×5	×7	×4	×6

429	397	$3\overline{)1632}$
×37	×126	

$\frac{1}{3} = \frac{?}{21}$ $\frac{9}{10} = \frac{?}{20}$ $10 \times 1/2 =$

$\frac{7}{8} = \frac{?}{16}$ $\frac{4}{5} = \frac{?}{30}$ $12 \times 1/3 =$

$\frac{1}{2} \times \frac{1}{5} =$ $\frac{3}{4} - \frac{5}{9} =$ $\frac{9}{10} - \frac{3}{3} =$

$$\frac{3}{4} \times \frac{8}{9} = \qquad \frac{5}{8} - \frac{3}{4} = \qquad \frac{7}{8} - \frac{3}{4} =$$

$$
\begin{array}{r} 3.2 \\ \times 0.7 \\ \hline \end{array}
\qquad
\begin{array}{r} 0.65 \\ \times 0.04 \\ \hline \end{array}
\qquad
\begin{array}{r} 8.6 \\ \times 2.5 \\ \hline \end{array}
\qquad
\begin{array}{r} 7.21 \\ \times 8.6 \\ \hline \end{array}
$$

$$2.5\overline{)625} \qquad 0.71\overline{)3.337} \qquad 0.35\overline{)2.1875}$$

Story problems.

1. Leigh bought shoes for $13.64. She gave the clerk a $20.00 bill. How much change did she get?

2. Mindy's room is 9 ft. × 12 ft. × 8 ft. What is the volume of her room?

3. Heidi's garden is 10 ft. wide and 13 ft. long. How long is the fence around it?

4. Priscilla's letter to John weighs 2½ ounces. If postage costs 13¢ an ounce or any part of an ounce, how much will it cost to mail the letter?

5. Yvette had $12.00. She gave 4/6 of her money to her friend, Gina. How much money did Yvette have left?

6. Joey and Eddie have $13.00. They want to buy fair tickets that cost $.75 each. How many tickets can they buy? How much change will they have left?

Match the columns.

.375

10²

30° angle

cube

decimal

trapezoid

60° angle

radius

diameter

⅝

exponent

Draw a polygon.

Draw an equilateral triangle.

Draw an example which illustrates an *arc*.

Make up a problem for finding the perimeter of a rectangle.

Make a problem for finding the area of a square.

Make up a problem for finding the circumference of a circle.

Use this page to make up a test for your classmates.

Include several different kinds of problems.

INDICATION OF SOCIAL SENSITIVITY— PRIMARY LEVEL

> If you agree, circle YES.
>
> If you *do not* agree, circle NO.
>
> If you aren't sure, circle the ? .
>
> If you don't like the statement, cross it out and substitute a different question for that one in the spaces provided at the end.

YES NO ?   1. Most people are good.

YES NO ?   2. Laws are very important.

YES NO ?   3. The reason people hate other people is because they don't understand them.

YES NO ?   4. Children can help grown-ups make the world a better place to live.

YES NO ?   5. The most important member of the family is the father.

YES NO ?   6. Women are more important than men.

YES NO ?   7. Everyone I like likes me.

YES NO ?   8. My teacher likes me.

YES NO ?   9. I'm glad I live in the United States of America.

YES NO ?   10. People have to have wars to get what they want.

My own statements:

(You may add some even if you didn't cross out any of the others.)

YES NO ?   _____

YES NO ?   _____

YES NO ?   _____

YES NO ?   _____

YES NO ?   _____

For each statement you answered YES or NO, tell why.

THINK AND KNOW INVENTORY— INTERMEDIATE LEVEL
(An Indication of Social Awareness)

Complete each open-ended sentence to make it state something you either *believe* or *know* to be true.

- Write T (think) in the space before each sentence you think is true. (It is only your opinion that it is true.)
- Write K (know) in the space before each sentence you know is true. (You can defend it with facts or evidence.)

_____ 1. People are generally _____.
_____ 2. The purpose of schools is _____.
_____ 3. War is caused by _____.
_____ 4. Children are most influenced by _____.
_____ 5. Things that make people hate are _____.
_____ 6. Things that cause people to love are _____.
_____ 7. Prejudice is _____.
_____ 8. People use prejudice _____.
_____ 9. The worst thing about the world is _____.
_____10. The best thing about the world is _____.
_____11. The feeling of my classmates toward me is

_____.
_____12. Teachers are _____.
_____13. A family is _____.
_____14. Cities _____.
_____15. The most important thing in the world is _____

_____.
_____16. Children can be helpful to their communities by _____.
_____17. When I become an adult _____.
_____18. People work because _____.
_____19. One thing that ought to be changed about the way we live is _____

_____20. Writing answers to questions like this is ___

For each statement you marked T, tell WHY you
   think so.
For each statement you marked K, tell HOW you
   know.

ABOUT ME . . . PRIMARY LEVEL

My name is _____.
I live _____.
I like to _____.
My friends _____.
You should see my _____.
I wish I could _____.
My mother _____.
School is _____.
Sometimes, I think about _____.
My favorite things are _____.
We go _____.
Teachers are _____.
I hate _____.
I am happy when _____.
I feel afraid when _____.
I like to play _____.
Two questions I would like to ask my teacher are:

   1. _____.
   2. _____.

ABOUT MYSELF . . . INTERMEDIATE LEVEL

My name is _____.

If I could change my name, I would be _____.

I live _____.

I am very _____.

I get mad when _____.

I just love to _____.

When I am alone I _____.

I'm sort of afraid of _____.

I like to think about _____.

If I could have three wishes, I'd ask for . . .

     1. _____.

     2. _____.

     3. _____.

Most of my classmates _____.

You should see our house when _____

_____.

I wish you could meet my _____.

I hate _____.

My father _____.

At our house _____.

On the way home from school I _____.

I don't know why _____.

Everyday, I _____.

The worst thing that ever happened to me _____

_____.

I wish I knew _____.

I hope someday I _____,
Two things I would like to know about my teacher are

_____

and _____.

PART SIX

SHIFTING RESPONSIBILITY TO THE LEARNER

A. Beginning Steps—Kinds of decisions that could
be made easily by my students
now.

    1.

    2.

    3.

    4.

    5.

    6.

B. Responsibilities to be assumed more gradually
(and a suggestion for initiating the process with
each).

WHAT	HOW
1.	1.
2.	2.
3.	3.
4.	4.
5.	5.

C. Ultimate goals for the shift of responsibility. (What I want students to be able to do in the ideal situation.)

1.

2.

3.

4.

5.

6.

PART SEVEN

COLLECTING AND ORGANIZING INSTRUCTIONAL MATERIALS FOR CREATIVE CLASSROOM USE

—Send a "help" letter or newspaper to parents describing needed goods and services.

—Ask the school cafeteria staff to save cans, boxes, egg cartons, etc., for you.

—Save milk cartons and empty paper cups from the lunchroom.

—Enlist your friends, relatives, in-laws, high school sororities, etc., to be "junk bankers" for you. (Supply them with a list!)

—Leave your name and phone number at stores with large, colorful advertising displays.

—Ask your dentist or doctor to donate old magazines from their waiting rooms.

—Sponsor a "junk" drive once a month.

—Go on a "treasure hunt" with a list of needs.

HUNTING GROUNDS:
   drawers (especially kitchen)
   waste baskets
   recycling centers
   back rooms at grocery stores

attics, basements
alleys behind stores
garages—and garage sales
school storage rooms
carpet/wallpaper stores
ice cream stores
"Give Away" sections of newspapers

ORGANIZING AND STORING MATERIALS

Remember that your materials are useful only if you can find them when you need them. The resourceful teacher will be rewarded a hundred-fold by devoting a few hours to organization and convenient storage of instructional materials. A written record of what materials are available, where they are stored and the specific center or unit they are intended to serve will be highly beneficial. (Example follows.)

For Teachers

large artist's portfolio
suitcases
footlockers and trunks
large, flat cardboard storage boxes (collapsible when not in use)
large cardboard mailing tubes
bags with drawstrings (to be hung on closet hooks)
shoe bags
spindles
peg boards

recipe boxes
multiple skirt hanger (for hanging charts)

For Kids

large ice cream cartons
mailboxes
oatmeal boxes (stacked sideways and glued together)
cloth sacks
"portable" plastic buckets or dishpans (stackable)
shoe boxes
cigar boxes
manila folders
accordian-type folder with fold top and string

For Classroom Materials

stacks of cardboard file cabinets
cloth shoe holders
wire baskets (stackable)
½ gallon milk cartons hung on a pegboard
large tin cans
scrapbooks
carts (on wheels)
small buckets or baskets with handles (for crayons, scissors, pencils, brushes, etc.)
hosiery boxes
plastic chlorox bottles with necks cut off, handles left on
baby food jars/cottage cheese containers (for pins, staples, clips, stickers, etc.)

WHAT I'VE GOT AND WHERE IT IS!

Activity or Center:

Set Search

Concepts/Skills It Covers:

Counting
Grouping objects into sets
Intersection and union of sets

Materials Needed For Its Use:

grease pencils
yarn

Where It's Stored:

blue trunk — basement closet

When I've Used It:

Jan. '73   Dec.-Jan. '74

Comments About It:

Yarn needs to be reglued!

To the teacher:
    This sheet is designed to give you one way to keep track of the individual
games, centers and learning materials you have.
    Every time you obtain or make a new item, fill out a sheet and file it in
a looseleaf notebook. (See completed sample.) You will find this to be an
invaluable organizational tool!

PART EIGHT

NEW WAYS WITH OLD MATERIALS

Access to a wide variety of materials spanning several different achievement levels can be one of your greatest assets as you prepare to launch your learning centers.

Materials already on hand in your classroom may be just what you need to re-program for use in centers. The rule of thumb is to use what you have while you are busy collecting more and better ones. Before you know it, you will have added the role of "materials specialist" to the list of areas in which you are developing new competency.

Here are some suggestions for securing and using a wealth of materials to supplement those in your library and classroom:

1. Make full use of every opportunity you have to secure free and inexpensive materials. Many companies now produce special materials to be made available to schools at little or no cost. These include posters, booklets, a limited number of books, charts and graphs, pictures, films, film strips, slides, folders, special leaflets representative of products distributed by the company, experimental kits and many other clever materials. Generally speaking, these articles are colorful, attractive, very well done, and advertising is subtle and kept to a minimum.

A practical and easy-to-use handbook which is kept up to date is *Free and Inexpensive Learning Materials,* Division of Field Services, George Peabody College for Teachers, Nashville, Tennessee—(cost $3.50).

2. Use discarded textbooks to make "new" books for individual students. Place stories or sections of books in acetate folders to be used as "work books" or make attractive covers for them from cardboard, cloth, construction paper or oil cloth.

3. Collect catalogs! They can be used in math, social studies and other centers. A "browsing" center would be fun too. Ask your students to help you plan objectives and activities for such a center. You'll probably be amazed at their ingenuity. Don't neglect seed, jewelry, toys, sporting goods and other specialty type catalogs.

4. Ask children to bring their own books or materials from home to use in centers. They love to share, and you gain insights into student interests through the books they bring. It also provides readiness for discussions related to the care and treatment of books.

5. Magazines are wonderful! You can never have too many. Their uses are so evident it would be redundant to elaborate on them here. Just

for fun, see if you can make a list of 100 ways to use magazines in your learning centers.

6. Workbooks taken apart and used for specific purposes in the centers are more acceptable than when they are handed out on the first day of school to be completed page by page.

7. Have children bring snapshots of themselves from home (or if this is not possible, maybe you can make them in the classroom). Use these pictures as the focal point of basal readers you can write using a controlled vocabulary.

8. Collect scraps of carpeting to sew together to make free-form carpets for reading or "dreaming" corners.

9. Save styrofoam packing materials and plastic bags to use in craft centers for stuffing bean bags, dolls, etc.

10. Encourage children to bring in scraps of lumber, wood trim and other materials for the carpentry center. Oftentimes, fathers will become excited enough about this kind of activity to volunteer both materials and their services.

11. Never throw away a greeting card—nor allow any of your friends or acquaintances to. Their illustrations make wonderful covers for jewelry boxes, waste baskets, etc., can be reused with construction paper to make new cards and often provide just the right "finishing touch" for

scrapbook or notebook covers. They are nice additions to the creative writing or composing center and can be used in lots of other ways.

12. Use scraps of colorful cotton cloth or wallpaper to cover cardboard boxes for storage, to use as room dividers or screens.

13. Get your name on the list at your local appliance store to receive large boxes (such as refrigerator or freezer containers) to be used for cubby holes, thinking centers, puppet theatres or as covers for large construction projects that need to be protected.

14. Make a special collection of gadgets to use imaginatively with the overhead projector. An "imagi-center" where children can tell a story or create one of their own by arranging objects for projection will provide hours of joy and learning.

15. Place rice or beans in shallow cardboard box tops for young children to use as background to make farms for miniature animals, roads for tiny autos or seas for walnut-shell ships.

16. Have you thought of a travel center equipped with railway and airline schedules, atlases, maps and travel magazines?

17. A current events center featuring news magazines and one or more daily newspapers will be a welcome addition to the intermediate or jr. high setting.

18. All the wonderful paraphernalia for establishing a grocery store can be collected by asking parents to save cans, containers, etc. for students to bring to school. The store can be set up on tables, bookshelves or in the versatile cardboard appliance carton. A toy cash register and a dollar's worth of play money will put youngsters into a business resulting in art, math, social studies and language skill usage.

19. A box of colorful silk scarves will be invaluable aids to creative dramatics, body movement, and lots of other imaginative projects.

20. Drivers' license manuals will be much more interesting as supplementary readers for slow readers at the jr. high level than will Shakespeare.

21. A stack of fashion magazines for girls and an equal number of Popular Mechanics or Popular Science magazines for boys will be welcome additions to any "free reading" table in the jr. high or high school. (You might also add a Hot Rod and movie magazine or two.)

22. Almanacs are delightful to modern-day youngsters. Most bookstores have very inexpensive ones complete with quotations from famous men, recipes, jokes and other goodies.

23. A collection of hats will give hours of constructive pleasure to young children. They promote role-playing and spontaneous creative dramat-

ics, and can be used in many language development and social studies activities.

24. Inexpensive window shades are great for use in middle-of-the-room learning centers. Instructions or directions can be printed with magic markers and the shade rolled up until time for use, then unrolled. If desirable, a standing frame may be constructed from plywood with brackets for the shade to fit into so that it becomes a floor-standing chart. At other times they may simply be unrolled flat for table top use.

25. Styrofoam egg cartons make convenient containers for paper clips, straight pins, rubber bands and other small items necessary for completion of center activities. Ready access to materials of this nature cuts down on traffic from one center to the other and consequently helps students to complete projects in the most efficient manner possible.

26. Plastic dishpans, available at discount stores for less than one dollar, make excellent "tote trays" for storage of personal belongings. They are light weight, easy to carry and add color to the environment.

27. Plastic milk cartons may be washed thoroughly and used for paintbrush or pencil storage, filled with soil to make planters for the science center, filled with sand and covered with con-

tact paper to make book ends. They make attractive mobiles to hang from the ceiling too.

28. Intermediate or junior high pupils who are poor readers may profit by acting as teachers' aides to lower-grade teachers by clipping magazines and helping to mount and prepare materials for use in learning centers. For instance, a first grade teacher may need large, colorful pictures of animals or foods or children or machines. The student has a well-defined purpose, the motivation of a prestige job, and he can't clip many magazines without doing *some* reading!

29. Carpet scraps may be used to cut figures of animals, flowers or other shapes to be pasted to walls in classrooms where the acoustics are less than perfect. These shapes placed in strategic spots will help to muffle sounds of scraping chairs, happy voices and tiny feet in perpetual motion. They may also be used as "bulletin board" space!

30. Use an old briefcase to make a "sand-tache" case for children who need the kinesthetic approach to word recognition. Simply add several cups of sand to the case and shut it. Sand will catch in the inside pockets. When opened flat, two children can work at a time, placing word cards in the center "crack" to use as models for writing in the sand.

31. For a fresh approach to the old book report

routine, let children use magazine clippings and construction paper scraps to design brochures which can be used to entice their classmates to read their favorite books. They may follow the model of travel brochures by tempting readers to "visit" the place where the story happened. The project can be expanded into math and social studies areas with the addition of maps telling "how to get there," room rates, mileage charts, dates of special attractions, etc.

32. Capitalize on materials that already have students' attention—i.e., favorite comic strip characters (write directions on Snoopy's house or on Linus' blanket), the current cartoon heros and heroines, the pop singers and movie idols. Put messages in personalized mailboxes, hang them on kites, umbrellas and parachutes, pin them to mannequins and stuffed toys or write them graffiti-style on a wall or mirror, perhaps in secret code . . . in short—recycle the imagination!!

PART NINE

USING UNUSUAL SPACES AND PLACES

Capture your students' imaginations with a learning center . . .

on a lampshade
behind the piano
on a clothesline
in a large appliance box
on the ceiling (flat!)
in a tent
in a shoe box
in a series of manila
    folders
on an easel
on the floor
in a duffle bag
behind a table—
    tipped on its side
on a mirror
in a flower pot
under *your* desk
on a cork board
    (small, portable one)
in a bucket
in a bookcase
enclosed by hanging
    beads, paper chains
    or burlap

on a shower curtain
in the hall
on a beachball
in a suitcase or trunk
on a kite
hanging from a hall tree
    or coat rack
in a shopping bag
on a cube
on a round table cloth
in potato chip cans
in a recipe box
hanging from the ceiling
under an umbrella
in a barrel (side cut out)
under a table
on the underside of a
    table
on the side of your
    filing cabinet
in a loose-leaf notebook
hanging from your chart
    rack
in a bottle

in a large straw hat
on a mat
in a wine rack
in a coffee can
in a birdcage
in a 5-gallon ice
    cream container
    (stores GIVE them
    away!)
under a canopy
in a terrarium
in an oatmeal box
in a large drawer
in a picnic basket
on a window shade
on a scroll
in a violin case
in or on an old tire
    or inner tube
in an old picture frame
in your closet
under a blanket
in a pumpkin shell
in a sock or stocking
in a toy boat or car

on a cushion
in a rowboat or old car
    (out in the yard)
behind the door—or on
    the back of it
on a pizza board
in an old TV set
on the sides or insides of
    a wastebasket or
    laundry basket
in a cassette tape carrier
in an egg carton
hanging from a tree (a
    dead branch, please—
    planted in plaster)
in an attaché case
in an old lunchbox,
    mailbox or hat box
on the venetian blinds
in a lady's purse
on a screen
in a fish bowl
on a real live human body
in a carpenter's apron
in a bird's nest

PART TEN

CREATE-A-CORNER!

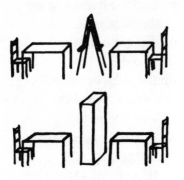

Place an easel between two desks.

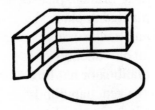

A tall cardboard box placed between two desks—two instant centers!

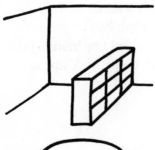

A cozy reading corner— just bookcases and a round rug—and books, of course!

A single bookcase against a wall in this fashion creates a private cache for study or projects.

Under a big round table is the perfect "creative thinking center"!

One/four centers can be created by placing a cardboard box in the center of a table. Place instructions on all four sides.

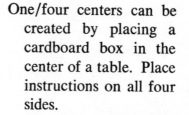

Ever thought of writing instructions on the ceiling?

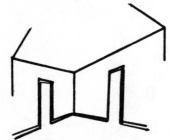

Don't ignore the space on the back of pianos, bookcases and teachers' desks.

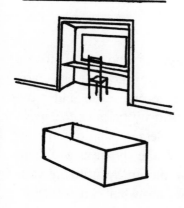

Transform the inside of a closet or cupboard into a study garret.

Use large appliance boxes covered with contact paper for storage, table space or covering projetcs spread on the floor.

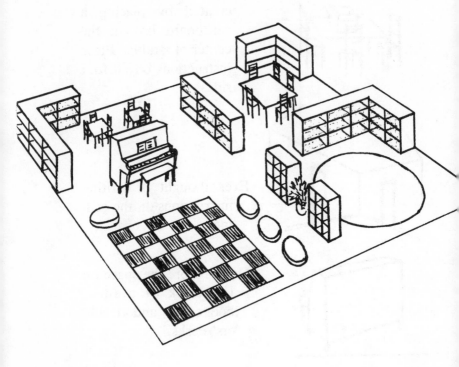

Does this arrangement appear too good to be true??? It may be impossible to imitate in every classroom, but the concept is a viable one, even under the least likely conditions. Top priority belongs to *space*. Furniture and equipment play lesser positions of importance. Storage is usually the biggest problem. "Saving" may be kept at a minimum by utilizing storage space outside the classroom whenever possible.

How much of this creative classroom arrangement could
be adapted to your own situation?

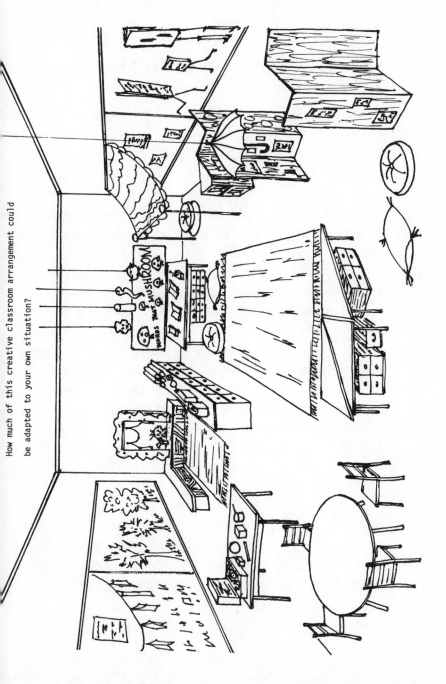

PART ELEVEN

CREATIVE APPROACHES TO RECORD KEEPING

Students and teachers alike will enjoy learning centers more when the stereotype approaches to record keeping which can be so deadening are replaced by more creative ones.

In devising records, you will want to keep in mind the need to help children *plan* their daily activities as well as to *evaluate* and *summarize* them at the end of the day. In addition to daily activity records, provisions ought to be made for evaluation covering longer periods of time, such as a three-day period, a week, or for more mature, self-directed students, as long as two weeks.

As is true in every phase of learning center planning, students should be involved as much as possible in the development of the records they will use. If the personalized approach is to succeed to the extent that the learner actually does assume responsibility for his own learning, then he, of all people, will be concerned with maintaining "balance" in his academic endeavors.

Many teachers have found that, while involving students in the development and use of records used to check and evaluate individual progress does not completely solve the problem of selection and quality completion of activities, it does encourage growth in self-direction. The question of children's honesty in marking records accurately continues to plague some teachers. Others feel that the quality of the learning experience and the intellectual stimulation gained from "children on their own" is of more importance.

The main purpose of records is to enable both teachers and students to keep track, with a minimum expenditure of time and effort, of the learning taking place in order that new activities can be planned on that basis. The simplest methods possible are the best ones, and when they can be "fun" at the same time, their use is enhanced greatly.

The following models are offered here merely as suggestions. You and your students will think of many that will be more appropriate to your setting.

Achievement Ships A'Sail on the Sea of Learning

Use the following pattern to make a ship for each child each day. The range of desired center activities may be pre-printed on the sail, so that it becomes a checklist for students to check off those centers in which they have worked during the day. More mature children, on the other hand, might write their own records as they see it. By using white paper for the sail, the back becomes available for special notes related to the progress record.

A large manipulative bulletin board, prepared in a convenient spot, offers a "sea" upon which each child may set his ship a'sail at the end of each school day. At the same time, he may pick up the next day's ship and plan then and there (as he pins his "today" ship in place) what his activities for tomorrow are to be.

At the end of the week, an interesting art project can be enjoyed as individual students collect their

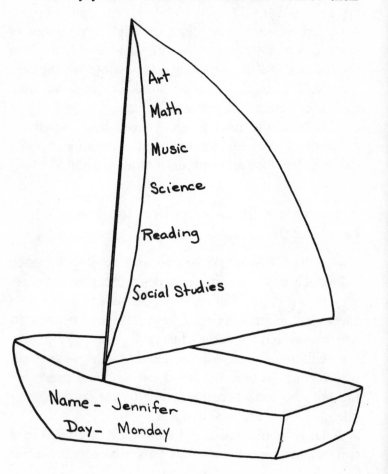

five ships from the board to arrange and paste on a "sea" of their own creation (could be tempera or finger-painted, construction or tissue paper or any other medium that children think of). This weekly achievement record may then be taken home to be shared with parents.

Flowers for the Teacher

Cut flowers from colorful construction paper and mount on plastic drinking straws (prepare one for each student). On each flower print symbols for the center activities for the week to form a checklist. Students check the date of completion of the activity on their flower. At the end of the week, students may place their flower in a specially prepared flower pot filled with sand or shredded styrofoam. An attractive flower pot with a few sprigs of artificial ivy or green leaves to provide interest will encourage students to want to fill their checklist in the best manner possible, especially if it occupies a place of honor on the teacher's desk the following Monday.

(A special flower pot prepared in this manner could be a great selling gimmick when presented as a gift to a still-doubting principal or supervisor.)

Nail-It-Down File

For more mature pupils, capable of planning and following through independent activities on their own for longer periods of time, a fine system for accounting for their time can be achieved very simply. A desk-top file may be made from a square of plywood large enough to securely support a large nail, driven upright through the board. Squares of paper, color-coded to denote areas of the curriculum (such as science, social studies, reading, etc.) may then be made available in each learning center. Students may record the amount and way they spend time in each center, carry it back to their own "Nail-It-Down File" and file it for future reference simply by placing the paper on the nail. At the end of the week, they have a true account-ing of how they have spent their time. These records may be tabulated and transmitted to a master record to be shared in conference with the teacher, or they may, in some instances, constitute all the information needed.

"Love Letters"

Weekly checklists may be given a new importance when they are printed on colorful construction paper folded to form a self-mailer, and pre-addressed to the teacher. Students are then asked to check them ap-propriately during the week, fold and seal on Friday, and at the end of the day put in a specially prepared teacher mailbox. Additional interest may be gen-erated through the use of colorful seals (such as flags, flowers, holiday symbols, etc., which are inexpensive and easily available at variety and school supply stores) to secure the privacy of the communication.

Students will also appreciate being asked to include a personal note to the teacher including any tid-bits they wish to share.

Slates

Had you thought of providing a small, inexpensive slate and chalk for each of your students, to enable them to keep an "erasable" record of how they spend their days? The "magic slates" available at ten cent stores are good for this purpose too. The freedom afforded students through a "swinging approach" to record keeping such as this one is sometimes just what they need to spur on that much desired self-motivation.

Progress Boxes

Every teacher moving into the learning center approach to individualizing instruction will be wise to make friends with the best possible sources. Cigar boxes are great! An excellent use for them is to make "progress boxes" to be kept by the students at their desks or cubbies. In these boxes they may keep recorded on slips of paper or index cards made available at each center, an account of time spent (and when appropriate, what was accomplished). These cards may be assembled at the end of the week to give a complete picture of the week's activities. Students will enjoy covering their boxes with contact paper or cloth and labeling them appropriately.

Big Records for Little People

Even very young children enjoy keeping records of how they spend their time. A daily record, using pictorial symbols to devise a checklist will be most rewarding and reinforcing to a young child. Once he has been shown exactly how to use it and the activities are geared to his interest and maturity level, he should have no difficulty in following through with it.

Help Wanted!

A clever approach to shifting room responsibilities
to students was devised by Mrs. Melody Moore and
Mrs. Lois Greenberg for use in their fourth-grade
classroom at Peabody Demonstration School. They
used the following poster to advertise job openings.

Choice Openings! Help Wanted! Apply now!

Efficiency Expert ——————————————————

Messenger ——————————————————————

File Clerk ————————————————————————

Art Custodian ————————————————————

Social Studies Custodian ——————————————

Language Arts Custodian ——————————————

Gallery Manager ————————————————————

Lost and Found Coordinator ————————————

Audio-Visual Expert ——————————————————

Thought Provoker ————————————————————

Ambassador ——————————————————————

Unusual Food Expert ————————————————

Book Organizer ————————————————————

Students used the following job application to "apply"
for the position desired.

JOB APPLICATION

NAME _____ JOB WANTED: _____

ADDRESS _____

AGE _____

DATE OF BIRTH ____

THREE REFERENCES (People who know you and think you are a good worker.)

    1. _____

    2. _____

    3. _____

EXPERIENCE (Any jobs you have done before like this one):

EDUCATION:

HOBBIES (And things you like to do):

WHAT DO YOU THINK ARE THE DUTIES OF THIS JOB?

IF YOU GOT THIS JOB, COULD YOU THINK OF SOME EXTRA THINGS YOU COULD DO THAT WOULD MAKE YOU AN OUTSTANDING WORKER?

WHY DO YOU THINK YOU WOULD BE GOOD AT THIS JOB?

WRITE ON THE BACK OF THIS PAPER A BIOGRAPHICAL SKETCH (tell about your life, your family, brothers, sisters, pets, where you have lived, what you do, some funny things that have happened to you and anything else you can think of).

INDIVIDUALIZED RECORD KEEPING

Your records need to show:

1. Objectives for the overall learning task
2. Step-by-step plans for completing the activities
3. What has been completed
4. Any desired evaluation of the work completed

Suggested Kinds of Records for Kids:

Folders of
   completed
   work
Check lists
Skills lists
Charts on desk
   (taped to it)
Assignment
   ladders
"Things I've
   Finished"
   sheets
Schedules for
   the day
   (or week)
Contracts

Graphs
Hats (with
   assignments
   clipped on)
Medallions (to
   hang around
   the neck)
Punch cards
   (center keeper
   or teacher
   punches as
   each activity is
   completed
Prescriptions
Independent
   study forms

Logs
Diaries
Individual file
   boxes
Scrapbooks
Notebooks
Library pockets
   located in
   strategic spots
   to hold cards
   containing
   records of
   pupil activity
Cassette tapes
Murals to
   denote
   continuing
   progress

(Let the kids develop the record-keeping forms that are convenient and workable for them!)

Suggested Kinds of Records for Teachers:

Center check sheet (at each center or activity)

Master chart of independent activities

Master list of skills (particularly math and reading)

Anecdotal card file (personal notes on each student)

Folder for each student (to keep notes, samples of work, etc.)

Prescription board or individual mailboxes

Individual conference schedule

Conference assessment sheets

Individual skill checklists

ONE TEACHER'S SYSTEM OF RECORD-KEEPING AND EVALUATION

I. BUZZ SESSIONS—At the beginning and end of each day, for general pulse and progress check, and to aid in setting and evaluating goals.

II. PUPILS' PERSONAL CHECK RECORDS—Pupils' own records of daily activities and progress. (See Examples)

III. MASTER CHART—Large, open record to which information is transferred by pupils or center keepers from the pupils' personal check records in order to provide instant reference as to progress toward goals for both teacher and students. (See Examples)

IV. ANECDOTAL CARD FILE—Teacher's personal record on each student. Contains notes, reminders and special information on academic progress, personal behavior, needs, etc.

V. PRE-CONFERENCE ASSESSMENT SHEETS —Aids students in preparing for individual conferences with teacher.

Teacher uses identical form to make notes and references before and during conference.

Student and teacher each keep own copy for reference. (See Example)

VI. INDIVIDUAL CONFERENCE—For most students, one weekly conference is sufficient. Others may need this private time with the teacher *more* or *less* often.

Individual Record of _____'s Work

Subject Area	Week ____			Week ____			Week ____			Week ____		
	Work Checked	Comments	Conference	Work Checked	Comments	Conference	Work Checked	Comments	Conference	Work Checked	Comments	Conference

To the teacher:

This is a record sheet which will help you keep track of students' progress. It provides (at a glance) a record of information and evaluation coming from your conferences with the student.

You might keep a copy of this for each student in a loose-leaf notebook.

NAME	Center A	Center B	Center C	Center D	Center E	Center F	Center G	etc.
Paul	ok	ok	ok			X		
Steve	ok	ok	ok	X			ok	
Mark		X		X				
Sheira		ok				X	ok	
Craig	ok							
Angelica			X	X	X			
Doug	ok	X	ok	X				
Mary Ellen	ok	X	ok	ok			X	
Yvette	X	ok			X	ok		
Heidi	ok	ok		X				
Priscilla	ok	ok						
Anna	ok	X				X	ok	
Julie	Independent Study							

In the left column: Names of all students

On the top line: Names of all centers

Markings: An "X" indicates that the center is not to be done. "OK" indicates that the center has been done.

No element of evaluation is intended.

To the teacher:
Using this device, the teacher is able to tell at a glance which students have been assigned to and have completed which center. Of course, the student keeps track of his own record sheet or prescription.

Name_____

PRE-CONFERENCE ASSESSMENT SHEET -- PRIMARY LEVEL

ABOUT MY WORK

Too hard!

_____
_____
_____

Too easy!

_____
_____
_____

Just right!

_____
_____
_____

ABOUT MY GOALS

Color the path as far as you think you were able to go

IN SCHOOL WORK

started	A little done	A little more done	a LOT done	almost all done!	All Done!

IN SHARING AND GETTING ALONG WITH OTHERS

want to	trying hard	doing OK	doing fine	doing great!	Fantastic!!!

PRE-CONFERENCE ASSESSMENT SHEET -- INTERMEDIATE

CENTERS

Center I enjoyed most_____Why?_____

Center I enjoyed least_____Why?_____

Center I feel helped me learn most_____

Centers I need help with_____

Centers I would like to pursue further_____

Questions/Problems related to centers:_____

_____

GOALS

I feel I accomplished my goals for this week.

Academic: _____ yes _____ no _____ partial _____?

Personal: _____ yes _____ no _____ partial _____?

I am most pleased with myself about _____

I am most disappointed with myself about_____

Goals for next week:

Academic: _____

Personal: _____

PERSONAL READING

_____

_____

* * *

I would rate my overall success this week as:

        Superior _____   Excellent _____   Good _____

                  Fair _____   Poor _____

Factors which may have influenced my progress are: _____

PART TWELVE

GETTING OUTSIDE THE CLASSROOM

The quality of open education programs is dependent on many direct personal experiences that take place both in and out of the classroom. By seeing, feeling and doing, children establish understandings and acquire social, intellectual and physical skills necessary for the development of strong self concepts. Going places, seeing and doing many and varied things are vital components of the successful learning center program. Children have more to read, write, talk and think about as they become more aware of the totality of the world in which they live. Exploration of the immediate environment through planned experiences which allow for individual experimentation and response provides stepping stones to expanded understanding of and appreciation for people, events and times beyond.

Good field trips do not necessarily need to be exotic or extensive; nor do they have to involve a great distance. Sometimes very simple excursions within walking distance of the campus, or even inside the school building, may prove to be very valuable experiences. The successful trip does however need to be carefully planned and carried out. Teachers sincerely interested in promoting learning on an individual basis, capitalizing on each child's past experiences and current interests will want to:

(1) Make a careful study of all places being considered as field trip possibilities *before* planning with the children, and visit the chosen site ahead of time.

(2) Check all aspects of the proposed trip with proper school authorities before plans for the trip are finalized.

(3) Plan the trip carefully with the children, being sure that they have clear, well-defined objectives for the trip. Only trips with a good "reason" should be taken.

(4) Be sure children have something specific to look for and that they remember what this something is during the trip (they will most likely need to be reminded).

(5) Establish behavior and safety rules during the planning. Make sure that they are realistic and that all children know what they are and are capable of following them.

(6) Secure written permission from parents or guardians *before* the trip.

(7) Devote adequate time and attention to evaluation and follow-up activities.

PART THIRTEEN

A MODEL LETTER—For Explaining the Learning Center Approach to Parents

Dear Parents,

Your child, his teachers and the students who share his classroom this year have already begun to experience an exciting new approach to learning. Well, actually, it may *not* be new, for it has been in vogue since the one-room schoolhouse days, but it probably has acquired some new characteristics since that time.

You may be acquainted with the terms "open classroom" or the "learning center approach," but you have probably already discovered that they do not have universal meaning. Perhaps the following brief explanation will give you some insight into this special kind of learning environment.

Simply, it is a plan of classroom organization that has been chosen—not because it is an educator's Utopian dream—not because it is the magical solution to all learning problems—not even because it is guaranteed to meet all individual learning needs. Rather, it is a more interesting and more personalized way of learning which we believe is more closely related to real living. Paraphrased, it is a chance for each person to be himself, learn all he can as quickly as he can— challenged, but unharrassed and unpressured—in the context of a living, working democratic community setting.

It certainly is not a license to idleness or "permissiveness." In fact, it requires a greater responsibility on the part of both student and teacher than any more traditional learning setting. The three R's become even more important. Basic skills are still systematically taught. But the exciting advantage of the learning center approach is that so many different kinds of learning experiences can be taking place at the same time! It gives us all more time to learn, and more room to live and enjoy learning!

P.S. This kind of community has room for parents too! Please plan to visit with us and watch us live and learn.

PART FOURTEEN

CHECKLIST FOR EVALUATING
INDEPENDENT ACTIVITIES

_____ Fits the growth needs of the students.

_____ Provides for a specific child-centered need.

_____ Is only one part of a plan of balanced learning experiences.

_____ Includes clear, concise instructions which are not dependent on teacher explanations.

_____ Specifies all reference and resource materials necessary for project completion.

_____ Provides for growth in study skill usage.

_____ Serves some valid educational purpose such as providing specific practice and drill, supplying evaluative material for diagnosis or extending learning experiences.

_____ Is presented to students attractively and interestingly.

_____ Includes evaluative criteria that is meaningful to students.

PART FIFTEEN

SELECTED REFERENCES

An Annotated Listing of KIDS' STUFF Learning Center Resources

For gaining understanding, developing readiness, creating the environment and moving into the Learning Center Approach:

Forte, Imogene, Mary Ann Pangle and Robbie Tupa. *Center Stuff for Nooks, Crannies and Corners.* Nashville: Incentive Publications, 1973.

This book contains more than fifty actual learning centers in math, science, social studies and language arts which can be used in either open space or traditional classrooms. Each model center contains performance objectives, an accounting of the materials needed and procedures for implementation. Coded student activity sheets on three levels of difficulty to be clipped out and reproduced for center use and illustrations and photos of the real life center in use are also provided. Perforated activity pages have a three-hole punch to make them easy to remove, reproduce and file in a loose-leaf notebook for later use.

Forte, Imogene and Mary Ann Pangle. *More Center Stuff for Nooks, Crannies and Corners.* Nashville: Incentive Publications, 1974.

This book contains more than fifty exciting new centers, much like the ones found in the original volume, with ready-to-use materials for instruction in math, science, social studies and language arts. Each model center contains a list of performance objectives, materials needed, procedures that will make the lesson come to life, student activity sheets on three levels of difficulty—to be clipped out and reproduced for center use, and illustrations of the center as it might appear when set up and operative. Perforated activity sheets are holepunched so they can be easily removed, reproduced and stored conveniently in a looseleaf notebook.

Forte, Imogene and Mary Ann Pangle. *Mini-Center Stuff*. Nashville: Incentive Publications, 1976.

Sixty-nine quick and easy self-contained activity centers for elementary grades. Every center is designed to be an easily portable, personalized learning center which may be used to reinforce skills and concepts in math, language, environmental studies or creative arts. Every center includes full student instructions and all materials for carrying out three or more related activities.

Forte, Imogene, Mary Ann Pangle and Robbie Tupa. *Cornering Creative Writing*. Nashville: Incentive Publications, 1974.

The authors have designed fifty-two illustrated creative writing centers to enhance and reinforce the more highly structured instructional learning centers presented in *Center Stuff for Nooks, Crannies and Corners*. These centers are planned to allow each student to work flexibly in keeping with his own interests and academic abilities. The appendix includes games to help students master basic skills and the mechanics of writing. Eighteen pages of special "Teacher Tactics" to help the teacher create an environment that will challenge children to write honestly, sensitively and beautifully are also included.

Farnette, Cherrie, Imogene Forte and Barbara Loss. *Special Kids' Stuff*. Nashville: Incentive Publications, 1976.

A simple format featuring easy-to-follow directions and limited vocabulary is utilized to teach or reinforce basic language arts skills or cencepts. Each learning experience is presented at three or more levels of difficulty, using a coding system which enables the teacher to quickly select and adapt experiences to meet widely varying readiness stages. Study projects, contracts, learning centers, puzzles, activity cards, stories and illustrated, reproducible work sheets all provide humor and creative opportunity for skill development on an individual or group basis.

Forte, Imogene, Mary Ann Pangle and Robbie Tupa, *Pumpkins, Pinwheels and Peppermint Packages, Teacher Edition*. Nashville: Incentive Publications, 1974.

This teacher idea book contains activities and centers for observing American traditions, events and holidays. The thirty-eight centers and more than three hundred and fifty activities have been designed to acquaint children with and develop appreciation for these special days and customs, providing enriching learning experiences in the academic content areas. Each learning center is completely illustrated and contains the following components: activities in communications, creative arts, environmental studies and quantitative studies; a puzzle or game, and a smorgasbord of "just for fun" ideas.

Forte, Imogene, Mary Ann Pangle and Robbie Tupa, *Pumpkins, Pinwheels and Peppermint Packages, Student Edition*. Nashville: Incentive Publications, 1975.

The two hundred thirty-eight ready-to-reproduce pupil pages are designed to accompany the activities presented in the hardback teacher edition. (This book serves as companion to but may be used independently of the teacher edition.)

For ideas, activities, techniques and procedures to meet individual student needs and interests:

Farnette, Cherrie, Imogene Forte and Barbara Loss. *Kid's Stuff, Reading and Writing Readiness*. Nashville: Incentive Publications, 1975.

This individualized, competency-based model for language readiness instruction features a simple management system based on an improved perscriptive teaching approach using sequentially presented activities. The back of each of the more than one hundred pupil pages, ready to reproduce and use, presents instructions for the teacher. The ideas, teaching strategies and teacher resources have been designed to make this book a valuable addition to the kindergarten, first grade or special education teacher's library.

Collier, Mary Jo, Imogene Forte and Joy MacKenzie. *Kids' Stuff, Kindergarten and Nursery School.* Nashville: Incentive Publications, 1969.

A collection of activities, songs, learning games, bulletin boards, learning centers, teaching techniques, recipes, resource materials and practical hints and suggestions for creative "thinking and doing." Two hundred thirty pages are filled with ideas for presenting basic concepts in language arts, science, social studies, math, art and music to young children.

Forte, Imogene and Joy MacKenzie. *Kids' Stuff, Reading and Language Experiences, Primary Level.* Nashville: Incentive Publications, 1974.

This book provides ready-to-teach reading, spelling, speaking, listening and writing lesson plans and ideas. Each activity is focused upon a specific language arts skill with step-by-step directions for both teachers and students, and explicit diagrams and illustrations for lesson presentation. Copyright reservations are waived on marked student activity pages so that they may be reproduced for class or individual use. Special "notes" for the teacher offer simple short cuts and bright ideas, and a very practical appendix includes bulletin boards, grouping plans, checklists, resource lists, evaluative techniques, etc. to help teachers spread the "icing" on an exciting cake!

Forte, Imogene, Marjorie Frank and Joy MacKenzie. *Kids' Stuff, Reading and Language Experiences, Intermediate-Jr. High.* Nashville: Incentive Publications, 1973.

Three hundred plus pages of explicit and practical instructions for presenting reading and language arts skills and concepts with creative flair are found in this book. Reading, spelling, speaking, listening, and creative writing activities for the "restless set" are presented with special instructions for tailoring ideas to the learning center approach. The appendix includes pointers and suggestions for record keeping, room arrangements, time schedules and bulletin board ideas.

Frank, Marjorie, *Kids' Stuff, Math.* Nashville: Incentive Publications, 1974.

This teacher's guide offers hundreds of activities, games, ideas, centers and bulletin boards for teaching math skills in both the traditional English and the new metric systems. Illustrations, patterns to reproduce, a comprehensive skills list, student activity pages and an illustrated glossary are designed to help elementary classroom teachers individualize math instruction.

Forte, Imogene and Joy MacKenzie. *Kids' Stuff Social Studies.* Nashville: Incentive Publications, 1976.

More than one hundred fully outlined and illustrated lessons and activities are non-rigidly structured to be compatible with and supplementary to established social studies programs, and include over eighty student activity pages, study guides, glossaries, board games, map jobs, contracts, independent projects, reading records, student and teacher references and a complete social studies check list to assess pupil growth.

Liu, Sarah and Mary Lou Vittow, *Games Without Losers*. Nashville: Incentive Publications, 1975.

This collection of teacher-made game boards, puzzles and manipulative activities for reinforcing math, science, social studies and language skills and concepts is arranged for use with a minimum of teacher guidance. Each game is pictured with easy-to-follow directions for construction by teacher or students.

Farnette, Cherrie, Imogene Forte and Barbara Loss. *I've Got Me and I'm Glad*. Nashville: Incentive Publications, 1977.

A self-awareness activity book with reproducible pupil activity pages. Each activity is designed to help boys and girls "sort themselves out," discover their strengths and weaknesses, examine personal preferences and explore their relationships with others. (Follows USOE Career Education guidelines.) Emphasis is on functional reading and communications skills.

Farnette, Cherrie, Imogene Forte and Barbara Loss. *At Least A Thousand Things To Do*. Nashville: Incentive Publications, 1977.

A career-awareness activity book with reproducible pupil activity pages, each designed to help students develop familiarity with the many aspects of the 'career world. Utilizing communications and functional reading skills, students learn to think of themselves as vital forces in the work world of the future. (Follows USOE Career Education guidelines.)

Forte, Imogene and Mary Ann Pangle. *The Magic Teaching Series*. Nashville: Incentive Publications, 1977.

> *Spelling Magic.* Activities, gimmicks, games and "tricky" ideas for making those old spelling lists and lessons more meaningful.

> *Comprehension Magic.* More than two hundred activities designed to teach basic comprehension skills. Simple, easy-to-follow teacher and student directions supplemented by specific skills purposes, materials listings and variations.

> *Metric Magic.* A collection of creative games, quizzes, puzzles and problem-solving activities designed to present metric skills and concepts in a meaningful, everyday setting.

> *Vocabulary Magic.* A teacher's potpourri of ideas, suggestions, games, puzzles, quizzes and other activities to encourage vocabulary development. Word meaning and usage, creativity, sensitivity, appreciation and vocabulary awareness are major focuses of attention throughout the book.

ADDITIONAL REFERENCES

Carswell, Evelyn M. and Darrell L. Roubinek. *Open Sesame: A Primer in Open Education*. Pacific Palisades, CA: Goodyear Publishing Co., 1974.

Chase, Larry. *The Other Side of the Report Card: A How-To-Do-It Program for Affective Education*. Santa Monica, CA: Goodyear Publishing Co., 1975.

Curwin, Richard L. and Barbara S. Fuhrmann. *Discovering Your Teaching Self: Humanistic Approaches to Effective Teaching*. Englewood Cliffs, NJ: Prentice-Hall, 1975.

Dunn, Rita and Kenneth Dunn. *Practical Approaches to Individualizing Instruction: Contracts and Other Effective Teaching Strategies*. West Nyack, NY: Parker Publishing Co., 1972.

Hertzberg, Alvin and Edward F. Stone. *Schools Are for Children*. New York: Schocken Books, 1971.

Holt, John. *What Do I Do Monday?* New York: E. P. Dutton and Company, 1970.

Howes, Virgil M. *Informal Teaching in the Open Classroom*. New York: Macmillan Publishing Co., 1974.

Kaplan, Sandra N., J. A. B. Kaplan, S. K. Madsen and B. T. Gould. *A Young Child Experiences: Activities for Teaching and Learning*. Pacific Palisades, CA: Goodyear Publishing Co., 1975.

Kaplan, Sandra N., J. A. B. Kaplan, S. K. Madsen and B. K. Taylor. *Change for Children: Ideas and Activities for Individualizing Learning.* Santa Monica, CA: Goodyear Publishing Co., 1973.

Kohl, Herbert R. *The Open Classroom.* New York: The New York Review, 1972.

Murrow, Casey and Liza Murrow. *Children Come First.* New York: American Heritage Press, 1971.

Oxley, Mary Boone. *Illustrated Guide to Individualized Kindergarten Instruction.* West Nyack, NY: Parker Publishing Co., 1976.

Perrone, Vito. *Open Education: Promise and Problems.* Bloomington, IN: Phi Delta Kappa Education Foundation, 1972.

Romey, William D. *Risk-Trust-Love: Learning in a Humane Environment.* Columbus, OH: Charles E. Merrill Publishing Co., 1972.

Silberman, Charles. *Crisis in the Classroom: The Remaking of American Education.* New York: Random House, 1970.

Silberman, Charles E. *The Open Classroom Reader.* New York: Vintage Books, 1973.

Stephens, Lillian S. *The Teacher's Guide to Open Education.* New York: Holt, Rinehart and Winston, 1974.

Taylor, Joy. *Organizing the Open Classroom: A Teachers' Guide to the Integrated Day*. New York: Schocken Books, 1972.

Weinstein, G. and Mario Fantini. *Toward Humanistic Education*. New York: Praeger, 1970.

Wurman, Richard Saul, ed. *Yellow Pages of Learning Resources*. Cambridge, MA: MIT Press, 1972.

INDEX

252